BUSINESS SPANISH

Learn Conversational Spanish
For Business Professionals

www.LingoMastery.com

ISBN-13: 978-1-951949-02-0

Free Book Reveals The 6 Step Blueprint That Took Students **From Language Learners To Fluent In 3 Months**

- **6 Unbelievable Hacks** that will accelerate your learning curve
- **Mind Training:** why memorizing vocabulary is easy
- **One Hack To Rule Them All:** This <u>secret nugget</u> will blow you away...

Head over to <u>LingoMastery.com/hacks</u>
and claim your free book now!

CONTENTS

INTRODUCTION

Hello student! We are proud to welcome you to **Business Spanish: Learn Conversational Spanish For Business Professionals,** a book we've produced for you to expand your abilities in communicating with business associates, banking contacts and company clients across the Hispanic world, helping you build your vocabulary and knock down the potential barriers that can stop you from getting your message across the world of finance and entrepreneurship!

We've mentioned it before in our books, but it must be *stressed* that over 570 million people speak Spanish across the world, with *21* countries across *5* continents (Africa, Europe, North America, South America and the Philippines in Asia) having named it one of their official languages - it is also the second most popular language in the United States, with 55 million Hispanic residents of the 327 million total speaking the Spanish tongue... we're talking about a language that is present pretty much everywhere you can go as a tourist, regardless of how far you are from its birthplace in Spain!

However, more importantly, your work will sooner or later lead you to come in contact with the Spanish tongue. It may be out of pure luck that you meet up with a regional manager from Mexico or Colombia, your boss wants to send you to Spain for a month or two or you may be importing an order from Argentina; it doesn't matter, you're going to need to be familiar with the vocabulary required to get your message across and accomplish the results you desire. In the fast pace of modern business, the knowledge of Spanish, whichever way you look at it, is as useful as knowing sales, finance or marketing.

The good news is, we've created this book with precisely that intention – to give you the knowledge you'll need to dominate in your market and broaden your landscape as an entrepreneur, investor or CEO.

Knowledge is power, and power brings money

Your service-based company has been reaching out for a while now since launch, seeking more and more customers in an increasingly bigger range of markets and countries. You, as the CEO, are certain that despite the rocky start, you're bound to find somebody interested in applying your technology to their business, when suddenly...

Your work inbox, so quiet since you set it up, suddenly receives a message. A company from Panama wants to connect after you sent them an initial contact email. They have English-speaking staff, but the CEO – who only speaks Spanish – wants to meet up with you. *Next week. That, or they're finding another company that can provide them with the same service at a higher cost.*

What do you do? How do you feel? Desperate, perhaps. Upset. You've lost the opportunity to start making business happen, and to begin making a larger income. But it doesn't have to be that way! You don't need to miss out on these opportunities, because no obstacle, whether big or small, should stop you from reaching your goals. Any businessman or businesswoman who is truly willing to learn new skills is already a few steps away from grasping success with both hands and running away with it.

There is simply no difference when it comes to learning Spanish.

Who we've created this book for

The world of business isn't just about producing something – services or products – and selling it to other people who need it; the world of business is about relations, trust, confidence and desire. It is about humans getting involved in solving problems that may be bigger than them, but which lead them to encounter amazing rewards that bring them happiness and prosperity, at least for a while.

Anyone in this world requires communication to solve these problems, and Spanish is one of the most common ways to accomplish it. You may be the CEO of a large corporation or the employee of a small venture, it doesn't matter: the skills you will acquire with our lessons will benefit you greatly in the coming years.

Plus, many doors will open for you when you can boast *"Speaks Fluent Spanish"* on your CV. Big jobs and big salaries await you, as will the big clients of your industry!

How this book has been structured for you

Business Spanish: Learn Conversational Spanish For Business Professionals has been written in a way that allows you absolute freedom in deciding what and when to learn, ensuring that you can choose from a variety of lessons and select what is best for your learning.

Each of the book's chapters is based on a situation that will inevitably present itself when doing business – these situations are exposed to the reader as conversations between two people, typically one businessman/businesswoman and another character, who want to solve a common problem found within the field of business.

The best news? You will be provided both a pure Spanish version and an English translation of each of these conversations, allowing you to read both and study what you need to know, observing the many differences and similarities between the two. There really is no way of getting it wrong if you pay attention to both versions; whatever you don't pick up at first, you'll soon handle further ahead. Such as how you learn to handle business with time, experience and the patience of getting around failures, it works the same way for Spanish learning.

Most importantly, however, is that we've preceded each conversation with a list of the toughest vocabulary you'll find within it, translating each word and/or expression into English and allowing you to practice what you're reading. This is a bonus, added to these conversations so that you can get the most out of them.

As for the content of these conversations, well... you're going to have to keep reading to find out, but they will have you covered in practically everything you'll need to succeed in business.

Final notes – Tips to getting the most out of our book

This book is as student friendly as you can imagine, with all of our efforts put forward to ensure an excellent and easy experience for anyone seeking to delve into the world of business in Spanish, no matter what age or fluency group they currently belong in.

Even so, some people may find that certain strategies will improve their learning when reading *this book*. We know that these tips will certainly enhance your results and allow you to develop your vocabulary to greater levels than ever! Let's start, then:

1. **Don't overdo it with the pressure.** Time is relative, as science has claimed, and you're not on a stopwatch. Go slowly, gradually and progressively while studying your way through this book; don't rush chapters just to get to a certain number every day, and keep in mind that it may be necessary to take some time redoing a chapter after realizing you couldn't handle it. This is no problem whatsoever; the basics will pretty much be the most difficult stage of learning, and you may need an immensely bigger amount of time during the initial phases than later on.

2. **Get the audio version of this book and take advantage of RwL.** *Reading while Listening,* an incredible method for learning new languages, has been proven at being crazily effective at building fluency and other cognitive skills in language learners. This is the magic of our book – it has been narrated to allow for an enhanced way of learning. Take advantage of this and start reading while listening today; a top-tier method to achieving your language goals!

3. **Grab your notepad (physical or digital) and start jotting down what you need to remember.** Some vocabulary will just not be easy to memorize, and you may face expressions that you had never ever witnessed before. If you think you need to keep something in mind for future reference, start taking notes and preparing your own checklists and materials.

4. **Partner up or form a study group for strength in numbers!** Studying as an individual is always courageous, but the absolute best results are achieved by forming groups and sharing the challenges you're facing on every level. Don't be afraid to come into contact with other students and face different issues as a community – this will only serve to strengthen your learning!

Having reached the very last of these tips and strategies, we reach the end of our introduction to this fascinating book. Now, we start with our real content in the form of conversations and lessons, and the only thing left for us is to wish you luck.

We can only tell you now to continue believing in yourself, having fun while learning and making the biggest effort you can to study Spanish. It'll all be worth it in the end as a businessman or businesswoman!

With all of that said, thanks for picking up this book! Time to begin!

CHAPTER 1

BASIC SPANISH LESSON

Every story must start at the beginning, and this particular book is no different. Though we were introduced to everything in the previous section, it may be tough to just get thrown into things right away; furthermore, there are tools that you may require to get started as a Spanish student that we wouldn't be able to provide in the upcoming conversations.

For this reason, we have split this chapter into three main sections, allowing students to begin practicing the most common aspects of conversation in written and spoken Spanish, with grammar, pronunciation and spelling very heavily stressed for improved results. Don't be intimidated – this section is for you, the student, and it will allow you to take on the bigger challenges further ahead!

So now, let's start with the first main section of the chapter: *starting a conversation with a Spanish speaker!*

Greetings and Introductions

Business involves a lot of communication. Shy people don't usually get very far in making money on the higher end of things, because the need for meetings and encounters ends up usually being crucial for the big-money deals and projects. There's just something more valuable about meeting in person and deciding something face-to-face that no computer program has yet managed to replicate, so we're still closing business deals the old-fashioned way: with smiles and handshakes.

For this reason (and more), you need to dominate the way you open up to a conversation in Spanish and start chatting with them. A grasp of greetings and introductions will be crucial if you want to make a great first impression and win your new friend over. In fact, confidence and self-belief are pillars in these types of encounters, and you will realize this soon as the conversation advances.

To begin a conversation with a greeting, many will use the expression *"Hola" (Oh-la),* which means *"Hi"* in English. This is a common mistake to make in many contexts, because you don't actively say *"Hi"* in Spanish when talking in formal or semi-formal situations. Business, especially, doesn't welcome this type of greeting, and it could earn you a frown or strange look.

Spanish has the habit of putting an emphasis of greeting somebody according to the time of day, which will be illustrated as follows:

Buenos *(Buey-nose)* / Buenas *(Buey-nas)* + Time of day

In this sense, **Buenos** and **Buenas** are masculine and feminine plural versions of *"Good"*. You may follow these by the time of day in which you are currently situated, in the sense of **Buenos días *(dee-az)*** for morning, **Buenas tardes *(tar-dez)*** for afternoon, and **Buenas noches *(no-ches)*** for the evening or night.

It is important to note that **Buenas noches** may also be used as a farewell for someone leaving or going to sleep; it is also important to observe that *días* is a masculine word and that both **tardes** and **noches** are feminine. Be wary with these genders, as they are very important when talking or writing in Spanish, and misgendering somebody is considered a big mistake.

Examples of these greetings:

- **Buenos días, estimado (ess-tee-mah-do).** = Good morning, dear sir.

- **Buenas tardes, compañero (com-pa-nie-ro).** = Good afternoon, co-worker (masculine).

- **Buenas noches, jefa (hef-ah).** = Good evening, boss (femenine).

You may follow up on these greetings with a *"How are you?"* or similar expression, further cementing the trust in this initial exchange. For example:

- **Buenas tardes, señora (se-nio-ra), ¿qué hace (ah-se)?** = Good afternoon, madame, what are you doing?

- **Buenos días, profesor, ¿cómo está?** = Good morning, professor/teacher, how are you?

As you may see when writing in Spanish, questions (and exclamations) require an opening question or exclamation mark to identify where you'll be asking or exclaiming something, and (despite not being very useful) must be written when you're creating a body of text.

Furthermore, you're going to want to keep an eye on accents (or tildes) when pronouncing or writing words because these will indicate where a vowel is stressed. Entire meanings can be changed from the writing of a stressed vowel, as in the case of este and esté, for example.

The next tool to identify is the introduction, or basically when you offer your name or identity to the person you're talking to. In other situations, this is kind of informal and may be considered a friendly afterthought; in business, however, you have to use this correctly and concisely if you want to accomplish anything.

In this sense, you can tell them who you are and what your occupation or role is in the following manner:

- **Buenas tardes, señor, mi nombre es...** = Good afternoon, sir, my name is...

- **Buen día, amigo, me llamo...** = Good morning, friend, my name is...

- **Buenas noches, señora, yo soy...** = Good evening, madame, I am (followed by either your profession or role)

- **Buenos días, joven (ho-ven), yo me dedico a...** = Good morning, young person, I am a... (followed by your profession)

A note to consider is that **mi nombre es** and **me llamo** are completely interchangeable for this purpose.

If you want to ask someone their name or profession, however, you can use the following questions:

- **¿Cuál es tu nombre?** = What is your name?

- **¿Cómo te llamas?** = What's your name?

- **¿A qué te dedicas?** = What do you do for a living?

- **¿En qué trabajas?** = What do you do for work?

This concludes the section on greetings and introductions, which we simply couldn't begin the book without. Next up, we have questions and requests – two tools in the language which you will certainly need.

Questions and Requests

There may be times when you need to either ask something or ask *for* something, as in any moment in life. We've all had the need to find out more about something we don't know about, but it can be even more difficult when trying to find out new concepts and terms in Spanish. Similarly, asking for something is a delicate subject, since you have to ask nicely and politely to avoid causing any disrespect.

To ask a question, there are several ways, but let's limit ourselves for now to the basic questions – *what, where, when, why and how?* These are illustrated in the following examples:

- *What? = ¿Qué?*
  - **¿Qué significa eso?** = What does that mean?
  - **¿Para qué se utiliza (oo-tee-lee-za) eso?** = What is that used for?
  - **Señor, ¿qué sucedió (sue-seh-dio) aquí?** = Sir, what happened here?

- *Where? = ¿Dónde?*
  - **¿Dónde es el encuentro (en-coo-en-troh)?** = Where is the encounter/meeting?
  - **¿Para dónde va el jefe?** = Where is the boss going?
  - **¿Dónde estamos ahora?** = Where are we now?

- *When? = ¿Cuándo?*
  - **¿Cuándo llegaste aquí (a-key)?** = When did you arrive here?
  - **¿Puedes decirme cuándo vamos a decidir?** = Can you tell me when we're going to decide?
  - **Me gustaría saber algo, ¿cuándo tendrás respuesta?** = I would like to know something, when will you have an answer?

- *Why? = ¿Por qué?*
  - **¿Por qué no ha llegado aún?** = Why hasn't he/she arrived

yet?

- **Dime (dee-meh), ¿por qué han bajado (ba-ha-do) las ventas?** = Tell me, why have sales gone down?

- **Quiero saber, ¿por qué llegaste tarde?** = I want to know, why did you arrive late?

- *How? = ¿Cómo?*

  - **¿Cómo podemos mejorar nuestros resultados?** = How can we improve our results?

  - **¡Increíble! ¡¿Cómo lo hiciste (ee-sees-teh)?!** = Incredible! How did you do it?!

  - **Tengo que preguntar, ¿cómo vamos a seguir (seh-gear) adelante?** = I have to ask, how are we going to continue forward?

Obviously, there are many more expressions to be used in this situation, but these are the bread and butter of all your question needs, and the ones you will be using most of the time.

As for requests, these will vary depending on who you are talking to and what you're asking for, but we will go over them briefly to help you out with these tools of Spanish. **¿Puedes?** and **¿Podrías?** usually start the request, followed by a **por favor** at the end, as you will see in the following examples:

- **¿Puedes (pueh-des) venir a mi oficina, por favor?** = Can you come to my office please?

- **Hola, ¿podrías (poh-dree-ass) cerrar la puerta? Quiero conversar sobre algo delicado.** = Hello, can you close the door? I want to talk about something delicate.

- **¿Podrías decirme cómo manejar (ma-neh-har) este problema, por favor?** = Can you tell me how to manage this problem, please?

As before, there will be many more situations that make you request something, but these will help get you off the ground. Now, however, we have concluded with this section. The next of these guidelines will provide you with farewells, so you can say goodbye and hope for a next meeting.

Farewells

Every conversation or meeting must come to an end, and this means that you will begin preparing your farewell, while hoping for a future encounter. In this particular sense, Spanish isn't all too different from English, and you should manage without having to learn too many things. Only the vocabulary itself is different, but experience will be enough to discover just how exactly you say "so long" in Spanish:

Adiós = Goodbye.
¡Chao! = Bye!
Hasta (az-tah) luego (loo-eh-go) = See you later.
Nos vemos pronto, señor = See you soon, sir.
Hasta la próxima = Until next time.
Fue un placer = It was a pleasure.

These are basically it, as you probably won't need other manners of saying goodbye to the people you work with (or for), as well as the fact that they will take you far on their own. Don't be afraid to use new vocabulary, though, and know that some people don't really mind if you're a bit *too* friendly with them. This can actually be well-received among some people, in fact, but be sure to get to know them before you overreach your limits!

Basic terms and vocabulary

The final section of our first chapter is about to begin, as we face the very last of what we need to teach you before you move on to our business conversations. In this particular part of Chapter 1, we want to provide you with the basic tools you are going to need if you want to communicate with others past the **"Hola, ¿cómo estás?"** stage, especially if you want to actually close a deal and make a new friend in the process.

Remember: the more words you know of a language, the more you know the language, and the quicker you will learn. In fact, the amount of vocabulary you're familiar with has been linked with the amount of a language you know, as well as the level of fluency you possess when reading, writing or speaking the tongue.

They may be simple, but many of these words and phrases will help get you out of trouble and allow you to let your new friends know what exactly you want or need, so don't discount them. You're going to need every single one if you want to succeed in business around Spanish speakers!

- **Basic verbs**

The first very simple vocabulary to be used in any language is the **"to be"** expression, which, unlike English, is actually two different words altogether – *"ser"* and *"estar"*. In the case of *ser,* we are talking about something the subject *'is'* in terms of personality, occupation, emotions or their description. In the case of *"estar"*, we are typically talking of their location, their temporal state or an action which is happening right now. Having cleared that up, let's start with examples, including how to use them depending on the pronouns:

Ser (soy, eres, es, somos, son)

Yo soy = I am
Tú eres = You are
Él es = He is
Ella (eh-ja) es = She is
Eso es = It is
(Nombre) es = (Name) is
Nosotros somos = We are
Ellos (eh-yoss) son = They are

Estar (estoy, estás, está, estamos, están)

Yo estoy = I am
Tú estás = You are
Él está = He is
Ella está = She is
Eso está = It is
(Nombre) está = (Name) is
Nosotros estamos = We are
Ellos están = They are

It's very simple: use the according pronoun and expression and start creating your own sentences. These are very basic terms, but let's also include other very common verbs: *can, want, need, give* and *take.*

Can (puedo, puedes, puede, podemos, pueden)

Yo puedo = I can
Tú puedes = You can
Él puede = He can
Ella puede = She can
Eso puede = It can
(Nombre) puede = (Name) can
Nosotros podemos = We can
Ellos pueden = They can

Want (quiero, quieres, quiere, queremos, quieren)

Yo quiero = I want
Tú quieres = You want
Él quiere = He wants
Ella quiere = She wants
Eso quiere = It wants
(Nombre) quiere = (Name) wants
Nosotros queremos = We want
Ellos quieren = They want

Need (necesito, necesitas, necesita, necesitamos, necesitan)

Yo necesito = I need
Tú necesitas = You need
Él necesita = He needs
Ella necesita = She needs
Eso necesita = It needs
(Nombre) necesita = (Name) needs
Nosotros necesitamos = We need
Ellos necesitan = They need

Give (doy, das, da, damos, dan)

Yo doy = I give
Tú das = You give
Él da = He gives
Ella da = She gives
Eso da = It gives
(Nombre) da = (Name) gives
Nosotros damos = We give

Ellos dan = They give

Take (tomo, tomas, toma, tomamos, toman)

Yo tomo = I take
Tú tomas = You take
Él toma = He takes
Ella toma = She takes
Eso toma = It takes
(Nombre) toma = (Name) takes
Nosotros tomamos = We take
Ellos toman = They take

These are among the most basic verbs, but they will get you far. You must practice them and include additional terms to form sentences of all kinds. These will help you further your grasp of the business side of things and allow you to negotiate with your associates and competitors. You can do it!

- **Basic vocabulary**

The next section of this chapter is the juiciest, considering what you're about to learn. While the verbs are greatly useful to know, you're going to need to know more than just the way to say "I want" if you want to work with other people at a company or get your message across to your employees, so we've prepared a list of the most common terms that will open the doors of Spanish to you when attempting to communicate.

Common business terms

empresa = company
compañía = company
empleo = job
trabajo = work
empleado = employee
reunión = meeting
inversión = investment
préstamo = loan
contrato = contract
ventas = sales
mercadeo = marketing

emprendedor = entrepreneur
retorno = return
factible = feasible
rentable = profitable
económico = economical
costo = cost
costoso = costly/expensive
barato = cheap
administración = administration
contaduría = accounting
contabilidad = bookkeeping
gerencia = management
gestión = management (verb)
superiores = superiors
director = chairman
ingresos = income/revenues
ganancia = profit
pérdidas = losses
tasa = rate
tarifa = fee
dinero = money
moneda = currency
pago = payment
transferencia = transfer
cheque = check
compra = buy/purchase
venta = sale
personal = personnel
capacitación = training
capital = capital
pasivo = liability
garantía = collateral
crédito = credit
deuda = debt
servicio = service
producto = product

Other basic auxiliary terms for business

vuelo = flight
chofer = chaffeur/driver
encuentro = encounter
viaje = trip
comunicación = communication
contacto = contact
oficina = office
teléfono móvil = mobile phone
secretaria = secretary (female)
mensajero = messenger (male)
atención al cliente = customer service
usuario = user
contraseña = password
reclutamiento = recruitment
responsabilidad = responsibility
esfuerzo = effort
alquiler = rent
traspaso = transfer

With the end of this list, we conclude **Chapter 1: Spanish Basics,** a section of the book built for you to improve your vocabulary before actually getting into the conversational content.

Hopefully, you shall begin practicing this content and making the most of it; you will use most of these words on a daily basis and will probably find many others to add to this list as you continue speaking Spanish. Our recommendation is that you copy this list of words somewhere else and practice each term with patience and effort, and you will soon notice how your Spanish fluency level increases.

In a final note, we hope you study these terms as much as you can before continuing to the next chapter – it's all going to get tougher from here on out!

CHAPTER 2

GIVING GOOD NEWS TO YOUR EMPLOYER

NUESTRA SUERTE HA CAMBIADO – OUR LUCK HAS TURNED

Vocabulary List

- **recibirme** = receiving me
- **Departamento de Ventas** = sales department
- **buena noticia** = great news
- **me encantaría oírla** = I would love to hear it
- **hacer contacto** = make contact
- **fabricante de plásticos y adhesivos** = manufacturer of plastics and adhesives
- **contratar nuestros servicios** = hire our services
- **se hará efectivo** = will be made effective
- **nuestro esfuerzo y el talento que tenemos** = our efforts and the talent we have
- **punto crítico** = critical point
- **menor punto en años** = lowest point in years
- **la sede de la empresa** = the headquarters of the company
- **nuestra filosofía** = our philosophy
- **materiales ecológicos con tecnología de punta** = ecological, cutting-edge materials
- **mejorar la calidad** = improve the quality
- **proteger el ambiente** = protect the environment
- **seguir los estándares y las regulaciones** = adhere to the standards and regulations

- **sus actuales proveedores** = their current suppliers
- **otros competidores** = other competitors
- **bono importante** = important bonus
- **pago adicional por empleados de excelencia** = extra payment for employees of excellence
- **el reconocimiento que tanto mereces** = the recognition that you deserve so much
- **estrategia para concretar futuros contratos** = a strategy to work out future contracts
- **generando estrategias** = generating strategies
- **¡enhorabuena!** = congratulations!

Spanish

Liliana: Buenas tardes, Francisco.

Francisco: Buenas tardes, señora Liliana. Gracias por **recibirme** en su oficina.

Liliana: Me cuenta el **Departamento de Ventas** que tiene una **buena noticia** que darme el día de hoy. **Me encantaría oírla.**

Francisco: Es cierto, señora. He logrado **hacer contacto** con una empresa importante, **fabricante de plásticos y adhesivos.**

Liliana: ¿Y? ¿Qué dijeron? ¿Están listos para **contratar nuestros servicios?**

Francisco: Sí, señora. Acabamos de firmar un contrato por más de cien mil dólares con ellos. ¡**Se hará efectivo** a partir de este fin de semana!

Liliana: ¿Cien mil dólares? ¿Estoy escuchando bien? ¡Espero que esto no sea una broma!

Francisco: No, señora Liliana. Gracias a **nuestro esfuerzo y el talento que tenemos** en nuestro departamento, hemos logrado concretar este enorme contrato.

Liliana: ¡Eso es increíble! ¡Felicidades, Francisco! Estábamos llegando a un **punto crítico**, ya que nuestras ventas estaban en su **menor punto en años**, pero... De verdad que ustedes hicieron magia. ¿Cómo lo lograron?

Francisco: Pues, mis compañeros y yo estuvimos hablando con ellos por dos semanas, y ayer viajé hacia **la sede de la empresa.**

Liliana: ¿Qué tal te trataron allá? Y, ¿qué hiciste para lograr que firmaran?

Francisco: Pues les expliqué sobre **nuestra filosofía**, además de los **materiales ecológicos con tecnología de punta** que usamos en nuestra empresa. Les dije que no solo iban a poder **mejorar la calidad** de sus productos, sino también **proteger el ambiente** y **seguir los estándares y las regulaciones**. Pero aún no estaban convencidos.

Liliana: ¿No? ¿Cómo hiciste para que se convencieran de contratarnos?

Francisco: Muy fácil: les hablé de precios. Cuando comparé nuestros precios con los de **sus actuales proveedores**, además de **otros**

competidores, terminé de empujarlos a lo que quería. Diez minutos después, estaban firmando el contrato.

Liliana: Vaya... creo que esto merece una celebración. Pero no solo una celebración; creo que tú y tu equipo ya merecen un **bono importante.** Este mes recibirán el **pago adicional por empleados de excelencia.** Es el mejor bono que ofrece la empresa, y me aseguraré de que lo recibas por dos.

Francisco: ¿Doble? ¡Muchas gracias! ¡Eso para mí es un honor! No tiene idea de cuántas horas de trabajo invertimos para que esto saliera como lo deseábamos. Incluso, pasé toda la noche de ayer preparando la presentación de hoy. Ni siquiera pude dormir bien.

Liliana: Pues este bono demuestra que nuestra empresa, y yo, te estamos dando **el reconocimiento que tanto mereces.** Espero que te sirva de mucho. Creo que estás entre nuestros mejores empleados, Francisco. Gracias.

Francisco: No hay problema, señora Liliana. Todo con tal de ver a nuestra compañía triunfando en el mercado. Es mi mayor deseo.

Liliana: Perfecto, tienes la actitud de un ganador y de alguien que realmente quiere vernos crecer. Ahora, ¿qué viene? ¿Ya tienes una **estrategia para concretar futuros contratos** o estás trabajando con improvisación?

Francisco: Definitivamente voy a seguir **generando estrategias.** Gracias por los cumplidos, señora Liliana. Seguiré siendo un ganador, ya verá. Bueno, regresaré al trabajo. ¡Gracias por recibirme!

Liliana: ¡Gracias a ti por la buenísima noticia y tu excelente trabajo! **¡Enhorabuena!**

English

Liliana: Good afternoon, Francisco.

Francisco: Good afternoon, Mrs. Liliana. Thanks for **receiving me** in your office.

Liliana: The **sales department** has told me that you have **great news** for me today. **I would love to hear it.**

Francisco: It's true, madame. I have managed to **make contact** with an important **manufacturer of plastics and adhesives.**

Liliana: And? What did they say? Are they ready to **hire our services?**

Francisco: Yes, ma'am. We've just signed a contract for over one hundred thousand dollars with them. It **will be made effective** from this weekend onwards!

Liliana: One hundred thousand dollars? Am I hearing correctly? This better not be a joke!

Francisco: No, Mrs. Liliana. Thanks to **our efforts and the talent we have** within our department, we've managed to make this enormous contract a reality.

Liliana: That's incredible! Congratulations, Francisco! We were arriving at a **critical point**, since our sales were at their **lowest point in years**, but... You guys really made magic. How did you accomplish it?

Francisco: Well, my team members and I were discussing with them for two weeks, and yesterday I traveled to **the headquarters of their company.**

Liliana: How were you treated there? And, how did you manage to get them to sign?

Francisco: Well I explained about **our philosophy**, as well as the **ecological, cutting-edge materials** that we use at our company. I told them that they weren't only going to be able to **improve the quality** of their products, but also **protect the environment** and **adhere to the standards and regulations.** But they still weren't convinced.

Liliana: No? How did you convince them to hire us?

29

Francisco: Very easily – I talked about the prices. When I compared our prices to **their current suppliers**, as well as **other competitors**, I finished pushing them to where I wanted them. Ten minutes later, they were signing the contract.

Liliana: Wow... I think this deserves a celebration. But not just a celebration; I believe that you and your team deserve an **important bonus**. This month you all will receive an **extra payment for employees of excellence**. It is the best bonus the company offers, and I'll make sure you receive it twice over.

Francisco: Double? Thanks a lot! That is an honor to me! You have no idea how many hours of work we invested for this to come out as it did. I even spent all of last night preparing today's presentation. I couldn't even sleep well.

Liliana: This is why the bonus demonstrates that our company, and I, are giving you **the recognition that you deserve so much**. I hope it serves you well. I believe you're among our best employees, Francisco. Thank you.

Francisco: There's no problem, Mrs. Liliana. Anything as long as I can watch our company triumph in the market. It's my greatest wish.

Liliana: Perfect, you have the attitude of a winner, and of somebody who truly wants to see us grow. Now what? Do you have **a strategy to work out future contracts**, or are you working on improvisation?

Francisco: I'm definitely going to continue **generating strategies**. Thanks for the praise, Mrs. Liliana. I will continue being a winner, you'll see. Well, I'll get back to work. Thanks for seeing me!

Liliana: Thank you for the amazing news and your excellent work! Congratulations!

CHAPTER 3

GIVING BAD NEWS TO YOUR EMPLOYER

UN AÑO PÉSIMO – A TERRIBLE YEAR

Vocabulary List

- **gracias por interrumpir tus actividades y venir** = thanks for interrupting your tasks and coming
- **reporte anual** = annual report
- **viendo bien de cerca** = looking very closely
- **las cifras suministradas** = the numbers provided
- **me siento un poco alarmado** = I feel a bit alarmed
- **nuestros ingresos han caído en un sesenta por ciento** = our revenue has fallen by sixty percent
- **una realidad que no puede ocultarse** = a reality that cannot be hidden
- **un momento económicamente terrible** = a terrible financial moment
- **aliados comerciales** = commercial allies
- **retirado su apoyo** = retired their support
- **definitivamente hay razones para preocuparse** = there's definitely reasons to worry
- **por qué no fui informado de todas estas cosas** = why was I not informed of all these things
- **me he enterado ahora** = just finding out
- **el Departamento de Mercadeo** = the marketing department
- **revertirlo** = revert it
- **una cuestión de vida o muerte** = a matter of life or death
- **la controversia generada por la reducción de personal** = the

controversy created by the personnel reduction

- **alegar que estábamos discriminando por raza y sexo** = claim that we were discriminating by race and sex
- **se esparcieron en el mercado como fuego** = spread across the market like wildfire
- **podríamos quedar en bancarrota** = end up in bankruptcy
- **reducción de personal** = reduce our staff
- **controlar los daños** = damage control
- **lucha contra la discriminación laboral** = fight against workplace discrimination
- **el apoyo a las minorías** = the support of minorities
- **trabajadores de distintos orígenes étnicos** = group of workers from different ethnic backgrounds
- **buena medida** = excellent measure
- **rescatar nuestra imagen pública** = rescue our public image
- **nuestra presencia en Latinoamérica ha disminuido** = our presence in Latin America has decreased
- **¿a qué se debe eso?** = why is that happening?
- **reduciendo el precio** = reducing the prices
- **llegar a los sectores más populares** = reach more popular sectors
- **cuestión de que hagamos ofertas y promociones** = we start making offers and discounts
- **no tema por eso** = don't fear for that
- **cambiando la suerte** = changing the luck
- **no puedo descuidarme** = I can't neglect it
- **contacto que llamar** = contact I can call
- **inversión que hacer** = investment to make
- **recuperar la confianza que se ha perdido con ellos** = recover the trust we've lost with them
- **puedo confiar en ti y en tus habilidades** = I can trust in you and your abilities
- **esta reunión ha concluido** = this meeting is concluded
- **te deseo mucho éxito en estos tiempos venideros** = I wish you

great success in these upcoming times

Spanish

Michael: Buen día, Sarah, **gracias por interrumpir tus actividades y venir.** Toma asiento. ¿Quieres un café o algo?

Sarah: Buen día, señor Michael. No, gracias. Si me ha llamado para su oficina, imagino que se trata del **reporte anual** que generamos la semana pasada, ¿no?

Michael: Sí, imaginas correctamente. Estuve **viendo bien de cerca las cifras suministradas,** y la verdad es que **me siento un poco alarmado** ante lo que estaba leyendo. ¿Es cierto que **nuestros ingresos han caído en un sesenta por ciento** en solamente ocho meses?

Sarah: Sí, señor. Es **una realidad que no puede ocultarse** —la empresa está pasando por **un momento económicamente terrible**—. De hecho, muchos **aliados comerciales** han **retirado su apoyo** sin explicación, así que **definitivamente hay razones para preocuparse.**

Michael: Y, ¿**por qué no fui informado de todas estas cosas** con antelación? ¿Por qué **me he enterado ahora?**

Sarah: Simple, **el Departamento de Mercadeo** estaba evitando comunicar esto por si acaso podía **revertirlo.** Yo apenas me enteré la semana pasada, y ya podría decirse que fue tarde. Por otra parte, no es una noticia fácil de transmitir, así que eso podría explicar los motivos.

Michael: Demonios, ¡pero era **una cuestión de vida o muerte!** Bueno, déjame calmarme y pensar... ¿A qué se debe el retiro de apoyo de los aliados comerciales?

Sarah: Tiene algo que ver con **la controversia generada por la reducción de personal** hace dos meses. Los medios lo utilizaron para **alegar que estábamos discriminando por raza y sexo,** y estas noticias **se esparcieron en el mercado como fuego.**

Michael: Esto no es nada bueno. ¿Ha surgido alguna idea de cómo revertimos todo este desastre? **Podríamos quedar en bancarrota.** Ahí no habría solamente **reducción de personal**; ¡*todo* el personal sería despedido!

Sarah: Sí, estamos contratando actualmente a una empresa de mercadeo para **controlar los daños** y hacer ver al país, y al mundo, que estamos comprometidos con la **lucha contra la discriminación laboral** y **el apoyo a las minorías.** Pronto pasaremos a contratar a un grupo grande de **trabajadores de distintos orígenes étnicos.**

Michael: Perfecto, una **buena medida** para **rescatar nuestra imagen pública.** Ahora, tengo otra pregunta: veo que **nuestra presencia en Latinoamérica ha disminuido. ¿A qué se debe eso?**

Sarah: Es posible que nuestros competidores estén **reduciendo el precio** de sus productos para **llegar a los sectores más populares.** Creo que sería **cuestión de que hagamos ofertas y promociones. No tema por eso,** ya estamos **cambiando la suerte** de la empresa en esa parte.

Michael: Perfecto, pero **no puedo descuidarme.** ¿Qué puedo hacer yo para mejorar esas cifras? Tiene que haber algo en las ventas en lo que pueda trabajar. ¿Algún **contacto que llamar** o alguna **inversión que hacer?**

Sarah: Personalmente, pienso que puede comenzar a hacer contactos con los aliados y **recuperar la confianza que se ha perdido con ellos.** Si nuevamente los logramos convencer de que inviertan en nuestra empresa, los números volverán a como estaban antes. De hecho, con las estrategias que tenemos, pronto vamos a hacer que todas las ganancias sean *mayores* que antes. Ya verá. Se lo prometo.

Michael: Excelente, Sarah. Creo que **puedo confiar en ti y en tus habilidades** para esta tarea. Bueno, creo que **esta reunión ha concluido.** Gracias por asistir a mi oficina y brindarme esta información. **Te deseo mucho éxito en estos tiempos venideros.**

English

Michael: Good morning, Sarah, **thanks for interrupting your tasks and coming**. Take a seat. Do you want a coffee or something?

Sarah: Good morning, Mr. Michael. No, thank you. If you've called me up to your office, I can guess that it's about the **annual report** that we generated last week, right?

Michael: Yes, you're guessing correctly. I was **looking very closely** at **the numbers provided**, and the truth is that **I feel a bit alarmed** at what I was reading. Is it true that **our revenue has fallen by sixty percent** in just eight months?

Sarah: Yes, sir. It's **a reality that cannot be hidden** – the company is currently in **a terrible financial moment**. In fact, many **commercial allies** have **retired their support** without an explanation, so **there's definitely reasons to worry**.

Michael: And, **why was I not informed of all these things** beforehand? Why **am I just finding out?**

Sarah: Simple, **the marketing department** was avoiding communicating this in case they could **revert it**. I barely found out last week, and it could already be said that it was late. On the other hand, it isn't an easy piece of news to transmit, so that may be an explanation behind it.

Michael: Damn, but it was **a matter of life or death**! Anyway, let me calm down and think... what is the reason behind the withdrawal of support of our commercial allies?

Sarah: It's likely something about **the controversy created by the personnel reduction** two months ago. The media used it to **claim that we were discriminating by race and sex**, and these headlines **spread across the market like wildfire**.

Michael: This isn't good at all. Has an idea come forth about how we revert this disaster? We could **end up in bankruptcy**. Then we won't just **reduce our staff**; *all* of our staff will be fired!

Sarah: Yes, we are currently hiring a marketing company for **damage control**, and to help the nation and the world see that we're committed in the **fight against workplace discrimination** and **the support of minorities**. Soon we will move on in hiring a large **group of workers from different ethnic backgrounds**.

Michael: Perfect, an **excellent measure** to **rescue our public image**. Now, I have another question: I see that **our presence in Latin America has decreased. Why is that happening?**

Sarah: It is possible that our competitors are **reducing the prices** of their products to **reach more popular sectors**. I think that it's time that **we start making offers and discounts. Don't fear for that**, we're already **changing the luck** of the company on that behalf.

Michael: Perfect, but **I can't neglect it**. What can I do to improve those numbers? There must be something that I can work on in terms of sales. Any **contact I can call**, any **investment to make?**

Sarah: Personally, I think that you can start to contact the allies and start to **recover the trust we've lost with them**. If we accomplish convincing them to invest in our company again, numbers will return to how they were before. In fact, with the strategies we have in place, soon we're going to make all the revenue *bigger* than before. You'll see. I promise.

Michael: Excellent, Sarah. I believe **I can trust in you and your abilities** for this task. Well, I think **this meeting is concluded**. Thanks for coming to my office and giving me this information. **I wish you great success in these upcoming times.**

CHAPTER 4

CONFIDENT INTERVIEWS
SOY EL MEJOR PARA EL CARGO –
I'M THE BEST GUY FOR THE JOB

Vocabulary List

- **proceso de captación de talento** = talent recruitment process
- **directora de Recursos Humanos** = director of Human Resources
- **inmediatamente comenzaremos con la entrevista** = immediately begin with the interview
- **parece estar entusiasmado** = you look enthusiastic
- **leyendo tus documentos** = I'm reading your documents
- **¿qué te ha traído hoy a esta empresa?** = what has brought you to this company today?
- **existen muchas oportunidades para trabajadores de mi perfil en el mercado** = there are currently many existing opportunities for workers of my profile
- **esta empresa tiene una filosofía, una misión y una visión que se asemejan a lo que yo quiero para mi carrera** = this company has a philosophy, a mission and a vision that are extremely similar to what I want for my career
- **aportar mucho** = bring a lot
- **me gusta tu actitud** = I love your attitude
- **te sientas a gusto** = feel comfortable
- **¿qué experiencia tienes...?** = what experience do you have...?
- **qué tipo de proyectos has llevado a cabo** = what type of projects have you undertaken
- **me irá muy bien aquí si soy contratado** = I will have a great time here if I'm hired

- **he trabajado para una gran variedad de empresas Fortune 500** = I've worked for a large number of Fortune 500 companies
- **la última empresa para la cual trabajé** = the last company I worked for was
- **industria bancaria** = banking industry
- **cumpliendo con los objetivos. Me fui en busca de un nuevo reto** = while fulfilling objectives. I left in search of a new challenge
- **la recomendación de mis superiores** = the recommendation from my superiors
- **muy reconocida** = world-famous
- **¿en qué ambiente de trabajo te desempeñas mejor?** = in what work environment do you perform best?
- **me gusta que me dejen hacer lo mío** = I like to be left to do what I know
- **instrucciones iniciales** = initial instructions
- **luego me dejen trabajar sin problema** = then be left to work without issues
- **soy bueno trabajando en equipo** = I'm good at working in teams
- **solo en mi cubículo** = alone in my cubicle
- **acá trabajamos en equipo** = here we work in teams
- **¿sería un problema para ti acostumbrarte a eso?** = would it be a problem for you to get used to that?
- **estoy abierto a nuevas posibilidades y métodos** = I'm open to new possibilities and methods
- **asociarse a nuestro Departamento de Mercadeo** = work alongside our marketing department
- **podrías incrementar los resultados logrados en ingresos** = you could enhance our results in sales revenue
- **he trabajado a fondo** = I've worked in depth
- **podríamos hacer una campaña de mercadeo por correo electrónico** = we could do an email marketing campaign
- **me gustaría que acordáramos los términos de tu contrato y procediéramos a la firma del mismo** = I would like us to arrange your contract terms and sign it

- **comenzar a trabajar apenas pueda** = start working as soon as I can
- **¡gracias por la oportunidad, Mary!** = thanks for the opportunity, Mary!

Spanish

Mary: Bienvenido a nuestro **proceso de captación de talento**, señor... ¡Daniel González! Mi nombre es Mary Pérez y soy la **directora de Recursos Humanos** en esta empresa. Puede sentarse, ya que **inmediatamente comenzaremos con la entrevista.**

Daniel: ¡Hola, Mary! Bueno, me parece excelente. Estoy muy emocionado por esto, de verdad.

Mary: Sí, **parece estar entusiasmado**, y eso siempre es bueno. De acuerdo, comencemos ya, ahora que estoy **leyendo tus documentos.** **¿Qué te ha traído hoy a esta empresa?**

Daniel: Pues, la verdad es que actualmente **existen muchas oportunidades para trabajadores de mi perfil en el mercado** de la tecnología de información, pero **esta empresa tiene una filosofía, una misión y una visión que se asemejan a lo que yo quiero para mi carrera.** Pienso que podría **aportar mucho** a esta ambiciosa compañía.

Mary: Vaya, **me gusta tu actitud.** Bueno, me encanta que **te sientas a gusto** aquí en esta empresa. **¿Qué experiencia tienes** como diseñador de UX y **qué tipo de proyectos has llevado a cabo** antes de llegar aquí?

Daniel: Sí, creo que **me irá muy bien aquí si soy contratado.** En cuanto a mi experiencia, **he trabajado para una gran variedad de empresas** Fortune 500, como podrá ver en mi currículo. **La última empresa para la cual trabajé** estaba en la **industria bancaria** y estuve con ellos por dos años, **cumpliendo con los objetivos. Me fui en busca de un nuevo reto,** pero aquí puede ver **la recomendación de mis superiores.** También he diseñado numerosos sitios web, incluyendo el de una empresa manufacturera de automóviles **muy reconocida.**

Mary: Impresionante, parece que todos tus empleadores anteriores te recomiendan para diferentes cargos, incluso fuera del campo del diseño. Eso es muy buena señal. **¿En qué ambiente de trabajo te desempeñas mejor?**

Daniel: Buena pregunta. La verdad es que **me gusta que me dejen hacer lo mío,** que me den **instrucciones iniciales** y **luego me dejen trabajar sin**

problema. Soy bueno trabajando en equipo, pero soy aún mejor cuando me dejan **solo en mi cubículo** y con completa concentración.

Mary: Bueno, **acá trabajamos en equipo** prácticamente todo el tiempo, es algo de nuestra filosofía. **¿Sería un problema para ti acostumbrarte a eso?**

Daniel: No, no creo. **Estoy abierto a nuevas posibilidades y métodos.** No quiero ir en contra de lo que ustedes hacen acá, ¡para nada!

Mary: Perfecto, me gusta esa actitud. Bueno, y estoy viendo acá que tienes experiencia en ventas. ¿Podrías contarme sobre eso? Tenemos un tiempo buscando a alguien con tu perfil para **asociarse a nuestro Departamento de Mercadeo.** Trabajando junto a ellos **podrías incrementar los resultados logrados en ingresos** por ventas de nuestros productos digitales y suscripciones. Sería lo ideal.

Daniel: He trabajado a fondo con suscripciones y modelos de monetización digital antes; no sería un problema para mí. **Podríamos hacer una campaña de mercadeo por correo electrónico** que probablemente generaría grandes ingresos.

Mary: Vaya, Daniel, parece que sabes exactamente qué es lo que necesitamos y buscamos en este momento. ¿Puedes venir mañana? **Me gustaría que acordáramos los términos de tu contrato y procediéramos a la firma del mismo**, si estás interesado, una vez hayamos terminado. ¿Está Bien?

Daniel: Me parece genial, vendré mañana y traeré un bolígrafo para firmar ese contrato. Sí sería bueno acordar los términos y **comenzar a trabajar apenas pueda. ¡Gracias por la oportunidad, Mary!**

English

Mary: Welcome to our **talent recruitment process**, Mister... Daniel Gonzalez! My name is Mary Perez, and I'm the **director of Human Resources** at this company. You can sit, as we will **immediately begin with the interview.**

Daniel: Hello Mary! Well, that seems excellent. I'm very excited about this, to be honest.

Mary: Yes, **you look enthusiastic**, and that is always good. All right, let's begin now, since **I'm reading your documents. What has brought you to this company today?**

Daniel: Well, the truth is that **there are currently many existing opportunities for workers of my profile** in the information technology market, but **this company has a philosophy, a mission and a vision that are extremely similar to what I want for my career.** I believe I could **bring a lot** to this ambitious company.

Mary: Wow, **I love your attitude**. Good, I love how you **feel comfortable** here at this company. **What experience do you have** as a UX designer, and **what type of projects have you undertaken** before arriving here?

Daniel: Yes, I believe **I will have a great time here if I'm hired.** As for experience, **I've worked for a large number of Fortune 500 companies**, as you can see on my resume. **The last company I worked for was** in the **banking industry**, and I was with them for two years **while fulfilling objectives. I left in search of a new challenge**, but here you can see **the recommendation from my superiors.** I've also designed numerous websites, including one for a **world-famous** auto manufacturing company.

Mary: Impressive, it seems that all of your previous employers recommend you for various roles, including outside of the designer field. That is a very good sign. **In what work environment do you perform best?**

Daniel: Good question. The truth is that **I like to be left to do what I know**, that I receive **initial instructions** and **then be left to work without issues. I'm good at working in teams**, but I'm even better when I'm left

43

alone in my cubicle and with absolute concentration.

Mary: Well, **here we work in teams** practically all the time, as it is something within our philosophy. **Would it be a problem for you to get used to that?**

Daniel: No, I don't think so. **I'm open to new possibilities and methods.** I don't want to go against how you do things here, not at all!

Mary: Perfect, I like that attitude. Okay, and I'm seeing here that you have experience in sales. Can you tell me more about that? We've been looking for someone with your profile to **work alongside our marketing department** for a while. Working within them, **you could enhance our results in sales revenue** through our digital products and subscriptions. It would be the most ideal approach.

Daniel: **I've worked in depth** with subscriptions and digital monetization models before; it wouldn't be a real problem for me. **We could do an email marketing campaign** that would probably generate great revenue.

Mary: Wow, Daniel, it seems that you know exactly what it is that we need and what we're seeking at this moment. Could you return tomorrow? **I would like us to arrange your contract terms and sign it** if you're interested once we're finished. Good?

Daniel: It sounds great, I will come tomorrow and bring a pen so that I can sign that contract. It would be great to arrange the terms and **start working as soon as I can. Thanks for the opportunity, Mary!**

CHAPTER 5

RECRUITMENT PROCESS
LA CAZATALENTOS – THE TALENT HUNTER

Vocabulary List

- **tenemos que llenar varios cargos** = we have to fill several positions
- **estamos expandiéndonos** = we're expanding
- **tendrás nuevos roles y responsabilidades** = you will have new roles and responsibilities
- **¿ya tienes los currículos?** = do you have the resumes?
- **lo primero y principal** = first and foremost
- **identificar a los nuevos gerentes** = identifying the new managers
- **ellos son los que van a dirigir las nuevas direcciones que vamos a establecer** = they will be the ones who will direct the new managements that we'll establish
- **el perfil que deseamos** = the profile that we're seeking
- **que tengan amplia experiencia en el campo de la administración de personal** = that they have broad experience in the field of personnel administration
- **un nivel alto de liderazgo** = a high level of leadership
- **que hayan trabajado con videoconferencias** = that they have worked with videoconferences
- **que tengan dominio de las normativas de higiene y seguridad** = have dominance in hygiene and safety standards
- **asegurar que el personal respete las reglas** = ensure that the workers respect the rules
- **tomando nota** = taking notes
- **con respecto a los administradores o administradoras** = about the male or female administrators

- **necesitábamos personas jóvenes, responsables y con cursos realizados** = we needed young, responsible people with courses taken
- **los últimos programas de administración y contabilidad** = the most recent programs of administration and bookkeeping
- **los requisitos para los candidatos de empleados de reparto** = the requirements for the delivery employee candidates
- **hombres jóvenes con buenos expedientes y experiencia en el cargo** = young men with good records and experience in the position
- **que tengan su propio vehículo** = who have their own vehicle
- **que no les moleste tener un horario flexible** = who don't feel uncomfortable with a flexible schedule
- **ha trabajado como repartidor en tres empresas de comida y una de envíos** = has worked as a delivery man in three food service companies and one of packages
- **cinco años como coordinador de repartos en una empresa** = five years as a delivery coordinator at a company
- **lo dejaré a tu juicio** = I'll leave it to you
- **¿qué tal estamos en la búsqueda de los guardias de seguridad?** = how are we in the search for the security guards?
- **robos** = robberies
- **personal experimentado** = experienced personnel
- **antiguo policía** = ex-cop
- **con un amplio currículo cuando se trata de consultoría de seguridad, vigilancia y otros aspectos** = who has a broad curriculum when it comes to security consulting, surveillance and other aspects
- **aquí tengo una buena candidata para atención al cliente** = here I have a great candidate for our customer support
- **es proactiva, responsable y está dispuesta a trabajar bajo presión** = she's proactive, responsible, and willing to work under pressure
- **creo que es la indicada para el trabajo** = I think she's the right one for the job

- **entrevistas y pruebas** = interviews and tests
- **finiquitaremos** = finalize
- **una preselección de los mejores candidatos** = a shortlist of the best candidates
- **estarás a cargo de todo el proceso** = you'll be in charge of the entire process
- **¡manos a la obra!** = time to get to work!

Spanish

Alberto: Bueno, Emma, finalmente ha llegado el momento para el que nos estábamos preparando. **Tenemos que llenar varios cargos** de la empresa ahora que **estamos expandiéndonos** y, gracias a eso, **tendrás nuevos roles y responsabilidades.**

Emma: Sí, es cierto que ya hablamos de todo eso. **¿Ya tienes los currículos?** Voy a necesitarlos. **Lo primero y principal es identificar a los nuevos gerentes,** ya que **ellos son los que van a dirigir las nuevas direcciones que vamos a establecer.**

Alberto: Es cierto. Bueno, comencemos con ellos; aquí tienes los currículos. **El perfil que deseamos** de los nuevos gerentes es **que tengan amplia experiencia en el campo de la administración de personal, un nivel alto de liderazgo** y **que hayan trabajado con videoconferencias.** También necesitamos **que tengan dominio de las normativas de higiene y seguridad,** para que puedan **asegurar que el personal respete las reglas.**

Emma: De acuerdo, estoy **tomando nota.** Y, **¿con respecto a los administradores o administradoras?** Creo recordar que decías que **necesitábamos personas jóvenes, responsables y con cursos realizados** en **los últimos programas de administración y contabilidad.** ¿Cierto?

Alberto: Exactamente, Emma. ¿Tienes anotados **los requisitos para los candidatos de empleados de reparto?**

Emma: Sí, estamos buscando **hombres jóvenes, con buenos expedientes y experiencia en el cargo.** Necesitamos personas **que tengan su propio vehículo** y **que no les moleste tener un horario flexible.** Me gusta la idea de estos dos: este **ha trabajado como repartidor en tres empresas de comida y una de envíos,** y este estuvo **cinco años como coordinador de repartos en una empresa.**

Alberto: Suenan bien, **lo dejaré a tu juicio.** Y, **¿qué tal estamos en la búsqueda de los guardias de seguridad?** Recuerda que en esta zona a veces hay **robos,** así que necesitamos **personal experimentado,** alguien serio y con un buen expediente.

Emma: Es cierto. Bueno, estoy viendo a un hombre acá: **antiguo policía** y **con un amplio currículo cuando se trata de consultoría de seguridad, vigilancia y otros aspectos.** Creo que podría servirnos.

Alberto: Perfecto. **Aquí tengo una buena candidata para atención al cliente.** **Es proactiva, responsable y está dispuesta a trabajar bajo presión,** según la recomendación que le hizo su último jefe. **Creo que es la indicada para el trabajo.**

Emma: Me parece bien. ¿Cuándo comenzaremos con las **entrevistas y pruebas** para emplear a estas personas? Es importante para mí saber cuál estrategia voy a aplicar para seleccionar entre los candidatos.

Alberto: Creo que este fin de semana **finiquitaremos** los detalles finales. Es la primera vez que realizamos un **proceso de captación de talento** de este tamaño. ¿Estás preparada?

Emma: Siempre lo estoy, Alberto. Para eso estoy acá, cuenta conmigo.

Alberto: Eso es lo que quería escuchar. Bueno, te doy dos días para que construyas **una preselección de los mejores candidatos. Estarás a cargo de todo el proceso** y sé que harás un excelente trabajo.

Emma: ¡Muchas gracias, Alberto! ¡Así será! Ahora, ¡**manos a la obra**!

English

Alberto: Well Emma, the moment for which we were preparing ourselves has finally arrived. **We have to fill several positions** within the company now that **we're expanding,** and thanks to that **you will have new roles and responsibilities.**

Emma: Yes, it's true that we've already talked about all of that. **Do you have the resumes?** I'm going to need them. **First and foremost** is **identifying the new managers,** because **they will be the ones who will direct the new managements that we'll establish.**

Alberto: True. Fine, let's start with them; here are the resumes. **The profile that we're seeking** of the new managers is **that they have broad experience in the field of personnel administration, a high level of leadership** and **that they have worked with videoconferences.** We also need them to **have dominance in hygiene and safety standards,** so that they can **ensure that the workers respect the rules.**

Emma: Alright, I'm **taking notes** now. And what **about the male or female administrators?** I think I can remember you saying that **we needed young, responsible people with courses taken** in **the most recent programs of administration and bookkeeping.** Correct?

Alberto: Exactly, Emma. Have you written down **the requirements for the delivery employee candidates?**

Emma: Yes, we are looking for **young men with good records and experience in the position.** We need people **who have their own vehicle** and **who don't feel uncomfortable with a flexible schedule.** I like the idea of these two: this one **has worked as a delivery man in three food service companies and one of packages,** and this one worked **five years as a delivery coordinator at a company.**

Alberto: They sound good, **I'll leave it to you.** And **how are we in the search for the security guards?** Remember that in this area there are **robberies** sometimes, so we need **experienced personnel,** somebody serious and with a good record.

Emma: It's true. Well, I'm looking at a man here: an **ex-cop who has a broad curriculum when it comes to security consulting, surveillance and**

other aspects. I think he could serve us well.

Alberto: Perfect. **Here I have a great candidate for our customer support. She's proactive, responsible, and willing to work under pressure**, according to a recommendation made by her previous boss. **I think she's the right one for the job.**

Emma: It seems great. When would we begin the **interviews and tests** to employ these people? It's important for me to know which strategy I'll apply to choose from among the candidates.

Alberto: I think that this weekend we'd **finalize** the last details. It's the first time we undertake a talent recruitment process of this scale. Are you prepared?

Emma: I always am, Alberto. That is why I'm here, count on me.

Alberto: That's what I wanted to hear. Okay, I'll give you two days for you to build **a shortlist of the best candidates. You'll be in charge of the entire process**, and I know you'll do an excellent job.

Emma: Thanks a lot, Alberto! That's right! Now, **time to get to work!**

CHAPTER 6

MARKETING
¡VAMOS A CRECER! – LET'S GROW!

Vocabulary List

- **estamos encargados del plan de mercadeo** = we're the ones in charge of the marketing plan
- **número de consumidores** = number of consumers
- **más licencias de nuestro programa a empresas grandes** = more licenses to our program to large companies
- **saber llegarles correctamente a estos clientes y convencerlos** = knowing how to correctly reach out to these clients and convincing them
- **nuestro producto es el mejor para sus necesidades** = our product is the best for their needs
- **cómo hacemos crecer más la marca de la empresa** = how we can make the company's brand grow further
- **gran número de ideas** = great number of ideas
- **invertido tiempo** = invested time
- **enfocados** = focused
- **incrementar el alcance de la marca en las redes sociales** = increasing the brand's reach on social media
- **los motores de búsqueda** = search engines
- **intercambio de ideas** = exchange of ideas
- **planteamiento de la estrategia** = exposition of the strategy
- **misión venidera** = upcoming mission
- **un plazo** = a deadline
- **abordar los problemas anteriores de mercadeo** = tackle the previous problems in marketing
- **nuestras habilidades especializadas en este campo** = our

specialized skills in this field

- **empresas fabricantes de productos especializados** = specialty product manufacturing companies
- **no tuvo sensatez** = did not have the sensibility
- **tenían miedo de fracasar** = were afraid of failing
- **publicidades pagas en las redes sociales** = paid advertising on social media
- **la cima de tu mercado** = very top of your market
- **pago a terceros** = payment to third parties
- **métodos gratuitos** = free methods
- **para que un sitio web gane mayor tráfico** = for a website to gain additional traffic
- **utilizando videos cortos de la marca** = use short brand videos
- **una gran herramienta para aumentar esos ingresos** = a great tool to enhance those revenues
- **publicar momentos especiales** = posting special moments
- **un detrás de escenas** = a behind the scenes
- **infografías** = infographics
- **guías rápidas ilustradas** = quick illustrated guides
- **nuestro propio programa de *podcast*** = our own podcast program
- **estudio de su perfil** = study of their profile
- **estudio de mercado en general** = market study in general
- **la entrega de mercancía** = handing out merchandise
- **venderlo de manera generalizada como mercancía** = selling it in a generalized way as merchandise
- **no dejar rastro de lo que hagamos** = without leaving a trail of what we're doing
- **no debería filtrarse al público normal y corriente** = cannot be allowed to filter out to the general public
- **una versión preliminar** = half-cooked version

Spanish

Tania: De acuerdo, Jim, ¡así que **estamos encargados del plan de mercadeo** de la empresa este año!

Jim: ¡Así es! Y, ¡qué clase de año tenemos por delante! Creo que podría ser el mejor que la empresa ha tenido, si sabemos aprovecharlo, ¿no crees?

Tania: Definitivamente, el **número de consumidores** en nuestro mercado solo crece y crece, y podremos vender más y **más licencias de nuestro programa a empresas grandes** sin pensarlo mucho. Lo importante ahora es **saber llegarles correctamente a estos clientes y convencerlos** de que **nuestro producto es el mejor para sus necesidades.** He estado pensando en **cómo hacemos crecer más la marca de la empresa,** y tengo una estrategia junto con un **gran número de ideas.**

Jim: Excelente, Tania. Yo también he **invertido tiempo** en esta tarea, durante mis momentos libres; ahora que estamos **enfocados** en esta parte del proyecto por completo, voy a poder pasar aún más tiempo dedicado a **incrementar el alcance de la marca en las redes sociales,** en **los motores de búsqueda** y en el mercado real allá afuera.

Tania: ¡Que bueno! Entonces, ¿será que damos por comenzado el **intercambio de ideas** y el **planteamiento de la estrategia** a utilizar para esta **misión venidera** que tenemos? Si hay algo que no quiero es malgastar nuestro tiempo productivo. Ya fue establecido **un plazo** para este proyecto y debemos respetarlo.

Jim: Eso es correcto: debemos **abordar los problemas anteriores de mercadeo** a través de un estudio de caso, y luego resolverlos con nuestra experiencia y, por supuesto, **nuestras habilidades especializadas en este campo.**

Tania: Sí, sobre todo nuestra experiencia. Creo que vamos a tener mucho éxito. Ahora sí, ¿qué piensas del proceso anterior de proyección de alcance? ¿Tuvo éxito?

Jim: No, creo que faltaron muchas empresas y potenciales clientes por contactar, especialmente en el caso de las **empresas fabricantes de productos especializados;** lo cual me hace creer que el departamento anterior al nuestro **no tuvo sensatez** para las actividades de investigación, y que quizás **tenían miedo de fracasar**. Un error común en nuestras oficinas. A mi parecer, es momento de comenzar a usar las **publicidades pagas en las redes sociales**. No hay nada como estar en **la cima de tu mercado**, ofreciendo los mismos bienes a un precio considerablemente mayor y, además, que te estén viendo todos los potenciales clientes en su sitio web favorito.

Tania: ¿Sí? Y, ¿cómo hacemos para explicarle estas estrategias a nuestros estudiantes y futuros trabajadores? Necesitamos establecer un sistema que llegue a todas estas personas y les explique cómo crecer en las redes sociales sin ningún tipo de **pago a terceros**. No solo hablo de publicidad como tal, sino de los **métodos gratuitos** que existen **para que un sitio web gane mayor tráfico**. Y es que, ganando mayor tráfico, tendremos la posibilidad de vender más. Una de las maneras sería **utilizando videos cortos de la marca**.

Jim: No solo videos, aunque son **una gran herramienta para aumentar esos ingresos**. Debemos considerar **publicar momentos especiales** dentro de la empresa; algo así como **un detrás de escenas** para que nos conozcan más. Eso es lo que pienso; además, sería excelente que creáramos **infografías**, **guías rápidas ilustradas**, y comenzáramos a grabar **nuestro propio programa de** *podcast*, todo con la intención de que la marca permanezca en la mente de todos.

Tania: Sí, entiendo. Me gusta la idea de enfocarnos también en la personalidad de estas personas que nos están comprando esos productos digitales. Necesitamos hacer un **estudio de su perfil** y un **estudio de mercado en general** para hallar la factibilidad económica de este producto. Vaya, Jim, sí que estamos adelantando muchas cosas juntos. ¿Crees que la campaña deba incluir **la entrega de mercancía** que dé a conocer nuestra marca de manera más efectiva?

Jim: Sí, recomendaría encarecidamente que hiciéramos esto y, de hecho, creo que cubriría la estrategia final a desarrollar para asegurar que nuestro producto esté en la boca de todos —**venderlo de manera generalizada como mercancía**, sin especificar lo que realmente está ocurriendo y **no dejar rastro de lo que hagamos**—.

Tania: Bueno, esto puede llevarse a cabo. Entonces, ahora que hemos establecido las estrategias y tácticas para el mercadeo, es momento de cerrar estas reuniones. Por favor, ten cuidado con lo que hagas o digas a partir de este instante, ya que esto **no debería filtrarse al público normal y corriente**, ¿sí? ¡Que nadie sepa lo que se intenta acá!

Jim: Entendido. Ahora, preparemos **una versión preliminar** de esto para la entrega, y vamos con todo con los puntos más comerciales para la entrega de mercancía. ¡Es hora de comenzar a crecer!

English

Tania: Alright Jim, so **we're the ones in charge of the marketing plan** for the company this year!

Jim: That's right! And what a year we have ahead of us! I think it could be the best that the company has had if we know how to take advantage of it, don't you agree?

Tania: Definitely; the **number of consumers** in our market only grows and grows, and we could sell more and **more licenses to our program to large companies** without thinking too much about it. The important thing now is **knowing how to correctly reach out to these clients and convincing them** that **our product is the best for their needs**. I've been thinking of **how we can make the company's brand grow further**, and I have a strategy alongside a **great number of ideas**.

Jim: Excellent, Tania. I've also **invested time** into this task in my spare time; now that we're **focused** on this side of the project completely, I'm going to be able to spend even more time on **increasing the brand's reach on social media**, **search engines**, and in the real market out there.

Tania: That's amazing! Then, should we consider the **exchange of ideas** and the **exposition of the strategy** to be used for this **upcoming mission** we have begun? If there's something I don't want it's for us to waste our productive time. **A deadline** was already established for this project, and we must respect it.

Jim: That's correct: we must **tackle the previous problems in marketing** through the use of a case study, and then resolve them with our experience and, of course, **our specialized skills in this field**.

Tania: Yes, above all our experience. I think we're going to have a lot of success. Now though, what do you think of the previous process of outreach? Was it successful?

Jim: No, I think that many companies and potential clients were not taken into account for contacts, especially in the case of **specialty product manufacturing companies**, which makes me believe that the previous department before us **did not have the sensibility** to do their research activities, and perhaps **were afraid of failing**. A common mistake in our offices. In my view, it is time to start using the **paid advertising on social media**. There isn't quite anything like being at the **very top of your market**, offering the same goods at a considerably higher price, and also for all of your potential clients to be checking you out on their favorite website.

Tania: Yeah? And how do we manage to explain these strategies to our students and future employees? We need to establish a system that would reach all these people and explain how to grow on social media without any type of **payment to third parties**. I'm not just talking about advertising per se, but the **free methods** that exist **for a website to gain additional traffic**. And it is through gaining additional traffic that we'll have the possibility of selling more. One of the ways would be to **use short brand videos**.

Jim: Not just videos, although they are **a great tool to enhance those revenues**. We must consider **posting special moments** within the company; something like **a behind the scenes** for them to get to know us better. That's what I think; furthermore, it would be excellent if we created **infographics**, **quick illustrated guides**, and that we began to record **our own podcast program**, all with the intention of the brand remaining in everybody's minds.

Tania: Yes, I understand. I like the idea of us focusing also on the personality of these people who are buying those digital products. We need to make a **study of their profile**, as well as a **market study in general** to discover the economic feasibility of the product. Wow, Jim, we're surely advanced a lot together. Do you think that the campaign should include **handing out merchandise** that could help get our brand known in a more effective way?

Jim: Yes, I would strongly recommend that we do this, and in fact I believe it would cover the final strategy to undertake in ensuring that our product remain in the public eye – **selling it in a generalized way as merchandise**, without specifying what is actually going on and **without leaving a trail of what we're doing**.

Tania: Okay, this could be done. So, now that we've established the tactics and strategies for marketing, it's time to close these meetings. Please, be careful with what you do or say from this moment on, as this **cannot be allowed to filter out to the general public**, yeah? Nobody can know what is being done here!

Jim: Understood. Now, let's prepare a **half-cooked version** of this for the submission, and let's go forward with everything on the more commercial points of the handing over of merchandise. It's time to start growing!

CHAPTER 7

STRICT DEADLINES
CAMBIO DE PLANES – CHANGE OF PLANS

Vocabulary List

- **Gerencia de Operaciones** = operations management
- **el encargado de elaborar los planos de diagramas de procesos** = the person in charge of creating the process diagram plans
- **planta de producción de plásticos** = plastics production plant
- **ingenieros de procesos** = process engineers
- **una de mis funciones** = one of my roles
- **tipo de documentos** = type of document
- **la sección de la planta** = the section of the plant
- **se va a construir próximamente** = will be built soon
- **¿o me equivoco?** = or am I mistaken?
- **no te equivocas** = you're not mistaken
- **necesitamos una serie de planos** = need a series of plans
- **vamos a requerir la representación gráfica** = we're going to require a graphic representation
- **las tuberías, los equipos, los accesorios y la red eléctrica** = the tubing, the equipment, accessories and the electrical grid
- **estas instalaciones** = these facilities
- **sí puedo elaborar todos estos elementos para usted** = I can create all of these elements for you
- **gerente regional de Procesos Petroquímicos** = regional manager of petrochemical processes
- **gran reputación como gerente** = great reputation as a manager
- **una gran trayectoria en la empresa y en el país** = a long track record in the company and the country

- **tener listos los planos para el miércoles** = I'll have the plans ready for Wednesday
- **necesitamos eso para el viernes, como máximo** = we need that for Friday, maximum
- **tienes dos días para culminar** = you have two whole days to finish
- **es más que suficiente** = it's more than enough
- **para que culmines el trabajo** = for you to finish the work
- **entregarlo a los constructores y los electricistas** = hand it over to the builders and electricians
- **no es razonable** = isn't reasonable
- **se hace muy cuesta arriba** = is too rough
- **exigencia** = demand
- **un área bastante grande y compleja** = pretty big and complex area
- **solicitarle al menos hasta el lunes** = request at least until Monday
- **debemos pedírtelo con tan poca antelación** = we must ask you for it with so little notice
- **de lo contrario** = on the contrary
- **nos atrasaríamos de una manera significativa** = we would be delayed significantly
- **posiblemente perdamos cantidades grandes de dinero** = potentially lose great amounts of money
- **no se puede negociar esta fecha de entrega** = this delivery date cannot be negotiated
- **trabajar horas extra** = work extra hours
- **no sé por dónde comenzar** = don't know where to start
- **puede consultar con mis superiores** = you can confirm with my superiors
- **esta fecha de entrega es demasiado cercana** = that delivery date is too close
- **voy a cumplir esta tarea a la perfección** = I'm going to fulfill this task to perfection
- **mal trabajo para terminar rápido** = a bad job to finish quickly
- **necesitamos negociar** = we need to negotiate

- **un trabajo acorde a lo esperado** = the job according to what is expected
- **proactividad** = proactivity
- **ascensos que vienen** = promotions that are coming
- **somos afortunados de tenerte trabajando acá** = we're fortunate to have you working here

Spanish

Elena: Buen día, joven. Me han comunicado desde la **Gerencia de Operaciones** de la empresa que tú eres **el encargado de elaborar los planos de diagramas de procesos** para la **planta de producción de plásticos.** ¿Es cierto?

Javier: Sí, mi nombre es Javier y soy uno de los **ingenieros de procesos** en esta área de la planta de producción. En efecto, **una de mis funciones** es crear ese **tipo de documentos.** Supongo que viene para que yo le elabore un plano para **la sección de la planta** que **se va a construir** próximamente, **¿o me equivoco?**

Elena: No, **no te equivocas.** De hecho, **necesitamos una serie de planos** para esa sección, ya que **vamos a requerir la representación gráfica** de las **tuberías, los equipos, los accesorios y la red eléctrica** que incluyen **estas instalaciones.**

Javier: De acuerdo, entiendo, es un trabajo grande. Bueno, lo cierto es que **sí puedo elaborar todos estos elementos para usted,** ¿señora...?

Elena: Mi nombre es Elena Gómez, soy la **gerente regional de Procesos Petroquímicos** en la empresa.

Javier: Vaya, mucho gusto, señora Gómez. La conozco por su **gran reputación como gerente.** He escuchado que tiene **una gran trayectoria en la empresa y en el país.** Bueno, puedo prometerle **tener listos los planos para el miércoles** de la semana que viene, creo que...

Elena: ¡¿Qué?! ¡¿El miércoles?! No, Javier. Entiende que **necesitamos eso para el viernes, como máximo.** Hoy es miércoles, así que **tienes dos días para culminar.** Pienso que **es más que suficiente para que culmines el trabajo** y tengamos eso en nuestras manos para **entregarlo a los constructores y los electricistas.** La verdad es que el miércoles de la semana que viene **no es razonable.**

Javier: Con todo respeto, señora Gómez, pero, para mí, **se hace muy cuesta arriba** esta **exigencia** de realizar todos los planos en dos días. Aún no tengo la información y, además, es **un área bastante grande y compleja.** Me gustaría **solicitarle al menos hasta el lunes** para esta tarea.

Elena: No es posible, Javier. Lamentablemente **debemos pedírtelo con tan poca antelación,** para este viernes, y *debe* ser ese día. **De lo contrario, nos atrasaríamos de una manera significativa** y esto afectaría mucho más que solamente la fecha de entrega. **Posiblemente perdamos cantidades grandes de dinero. No se puede negociar esta fecha de entrega.** Quizás debas **trabajar horas extra** para lograrlo, y se te compensarán.

Javier: Creo que lo más importante es ver la información preliminar. ¿La trae consigo? Sin eso, la verdad es que estoy un poco perdido y **no sé por dónde comenzar.**

Elena: Sí, Javier. Aquí lo tienes, en esta carpeta.

Javier: Oh... viéndolo bien, es demasiado para este viernes. No quiero que piense que no quiero cumplir con esta responsabilidad, ya que **puede consultar con mis superiores** y sabrá que puedo trabajar bajo presión, pero **esta fecha de entrega es demasiado cercana.** Necesito al menos un día más para poder decirle con seguridad que **voy a cumplir esta tarea a la perfección.**

Elena: Hmm... eres un joven sincero, ya que no cualquiera admitiría eso. Otra persona, quizás, haría un **mal trabajo para terminar rápido.** Veamos entonces, **necesitamos negociar.** ¡Ya sé! Tengo una idea que puede servirnos a ambos, pero tendrías que venir a trabajar un día extra. —¿Puedes venir el día sábado a terminar y entregar eso?—.

Javier: ¿El sábado? Mmm... Sí. Es una buena idea, al final de todo. Sí vendré a trabajar, y así hago **un trabajo acorde a lo esperado.**

Elena: Perfecto, Javier. La buena noticia es que tu **proactividad** será tomada en cuenta muy pronto para los **ascensos que vienen.** Excelente, te dejaré la información aquí y vendré mañana para traerte más. Muchas gracias, Javier. **Somos afortunados de tenerte trabajando acá.**

Javier: ¡Excelente, gracias a usted!

English

Elena: Good day, young man. I've been told by the **operations management** of the company that you're **the person in charge of creating the process diagram plans** for the **plastics production plant**. Is that correct?

Javier: Yes, my name is Javier, and I'm one of the **process engineers** within this area of the production plant. Actually, **one of my roles** is to create this **type of document**. I'm guessing you've come for me to create a plan for **the section of the plant** which **will be built soon, or am I mistaken?**

Elena: No, **you're not mistaken.** In fact, we **need a series of plans** for that section, since **we're going to require a graphic representation** of the **tubing, the equipment, accessories and the electrical grid** which **these facilities** include.

Javier: Very well, I understand, it is a big task. Well, the truth is that **I can create all of these elements for you,** Mrs....?

Elena: My name is Elena Gomez, I'm the **regional manager of petrochemical processes** at the company.

Javier: Wow, nice to meet you, Mrs. Gomez. I know about you thanks to your **great reputation as a manager.** I've heard that you have **a long track record in the company and the country.** Well, I can promise you **I'll have the plans ready for Wednesday** next week, I believe that-

Elena: What?! Wednesday? No, Javier. Understand that **we need that for Friday, maximum.** Today is Wednesday, so **you have two whole days to finish.** I think that **it's more than enough for you to finish the work** and for us to have that in our hands to **hand it over to the builders and electricians.** The truth is that next Wednesday **isn't reasonable.**

Javier: With all due respect, Mrs. Gomez, but to me this **demand** to finish all the plans in two days **is too rough.** I still don't have the information, and it's also a **pretty big and complex area.** I would like to **request at least until Monday** for this task.

Elena: It's not possible, Javier. Unfortunately, **we must ask you for it with**

so little notice for this Friday, and it *must* be that day. **On the contrary, we would be delayed significantly,** and this would greatly affect much more than just the delivery date. We would **potentially lose great amounts of money. This delivery date cannot be negotiated.** Maybe you should **work extra hours** to accomplish it, and you will be compensated.

Javier: I think the most important thing is to see the preliminary information. Are you carrying it with you? Without it, the truth is that I'm a bit lost and **don't know where to start.**

Elena: Yes, Javier. Here it is in this folder.

Javier: Oh… on a closer look, it's way too much for this Friday. I don't want you to think that I'm not able to comply with these responsibilities, since **you can confirm with my superiors** and you'll know I can work under pressure, but **that delivery date is too close.** I need at least a day more to be able to tell you with security that **I'm going to fulfill this task to perfection.**

Elena: Hmm… you're an honest young man, since not just anybody would admit that. Another person perhaps would do **a bad job to finish quickly.** Let's see, then, **we need to negotiate.** I know! I have an idea that could work for both of us, but you would need to come to work an extra day – could you come on Saturday to finish and turn that in?

Javier: On Saturday? Mmm… Yes. It's a good idea, at the end of it all. I'll come to work, and that way I can perform **the job according to what is expected**

Elena: Perfect, Javier. The good news is that your **proactivity** will be taken into account very soon during the **promotions that are coming.** Excellent, I will leave you the information here, and I'll come tomorrow to bring you more. Thanks a lot, Javier. **We're fortunate to have you working here.**

Javier: Excellent, thank you!

CHAPTER 8

ASKING FOR FINANCIAL HELP
¡SÁLVAME! – SAVE ME!

Vocabulary List

- **¡¿demonios, cómo voy a hacer ahora?!** = damn, what am I going to do now?!
- **estás un poco estresado desde hace rato** = you're a bit stressed since a while ago
- **no estoy muy bien, para nada** = I'm not in good shape, at all
- **no me están saliendo bien las cosas** = things aren't going well for me
- **muy mala noticia del banco** = very bad news from the bank
- **me negaron el crédito** = denied a loan I requested
- **estaban planeando cancelar mi tarjeta de crédito** = they were also planning to cancel my credit card
- **gastos médicos y las compras del hogar** = medical expenses and for groceries
- **mi esposa está enferma y que va a requerir tratamiento** = my wife is sick and that she's going to need treatment
- **es lo peor que me ha pasado** = it's the worst thing that's happened to me
- **evaluar tu caso** = evaluate your case
- **sacarte de apuros** = get you out of trouble
- **alguien cercano a ustedes que pueda hacerles un préstamo** = someone close to you guys who can loan some money
- **alguien especializado en este tipo de casos** = somebody specialized in these types of cases
- **cortar lazos con nosotros** = cut ties with us
- **no sé cómo voy a mantener mi hogar** = I don't know how I'm

going to maintain my household

- **ella fue a una organización benéfica** = she went to a charity organization
- **ellos se encargaron de brindarle apoyo** = they took charge of helping her out
- **la albergaron en sus instalaciones** = they housed her in their facilities
- **patrocinado por la organización** = sponsored by the organization
- **pudo recuperarse y pararse en sus propios pies nuevamente** = she managed to recover and stand on her own two feet once more
- **una vez empecemos a recibir ayuda, todo cambiará** = once we start to receive help, everything will change
- **no tienes idea de cuánto me has ayudado** = you have no idea of how much you've helped me
- **situación decente** = decent situation
- **tarjetas de crédito y los créditos bancarios** = credit cards and bank loans
- **pueden llevarte a la quiebra rápidamente** = it can quickly lead you to bankruptcy

Spanish

Vicente: ¡¿Demonios, cómo voy a hacer ahora?! Esto sí me va a poner las cosas difíciles.

Roxy: Hola, Vicente, ¿cómo estás? ¿Qué sucede? Veo que **estás un poco estresado desde hace rato** y me gustaría saber qué te tiene así. ¿Pasa algo?

Vicente: Hola, Roxy, ¿qué tal? La verdad es que **no estoy muy bien, para nada**. En cuanto a qué me pasa... son muchas cosas. Lo cierto es que **no me están saliendo bien las cosas** y, además, acabo de recibir una **muy mala noticia del banco**.

Roxy: ¿Sí? ¿Cuál mala noticia recibiste?

Vicente: Me llamaron para decirme que **me negaron el crédito** que solicité allí hace un mes y que, además, **estaban planeando cancelar mi tarjeta de crédito**, la que uso mensualmente para **gastos médicos y las compras del hogar**. Además, recientemente supe que **mi esposa está enferma y que va a requerir tratamiento**. Ahora, con esto, no será fácil lo que se viene. **Es lo peor que me ha pasado**.

Roxy: Eso es terrible, Vicente. Creo que hay que sentarse y **evaluar tu caso**. A ver, ¿no cuentas con familiares que puedan **sacarte de apuros**, ya sea con dinero o con medicamentos para tu esposa? Debe haber **alguien cercano a ustedes que pueda hacerles un préstamo**, por lo menos, o que pueda contactar a **alguien especializado en este tipo de casos**.

Vicente: No, Roxy. Mi esposa y yo no tenemos buena relación con nuestras familias porque ellos no estaban de acuerdo con nuestro matrimonio y decidieron **cortar lazos con nosotros**. De hecho, nuestros hijos no conocen a sus abuelos, y creo que esto seguirá así por mucho tiempo. La verdad es que **no sé cómo voy a mantener mi hogar**. ¡Tengo dos hijos pequeños!

Roxy: Bueno, conozco a alguien que estuvo en una situación parecida; **ella fue a una organización benéfica** y **ellos se encargaron de brindarle apoyo** por tres meses, hasta que salió de eso. **La albergaron en sus instalaciones**, le dieron tres comidas diarias y sus hijos tenían un transporte escolar que era **patrocinado por la organización**. Pasó los primeros días triste y avergonzada de estar allí, pero finalmente estaba feliz, sus hijos estaban contentos de nuevo y **pudo recuperarse y pararse en sus propios pies nuevamente**, como una mujer fuerte. En tu caso sería más sencillo aún, ya que ustedes son *dos* adultos, no una sola. ¿No crees?

Vicente: Oye, Roxy, eso suena como una muy buena noticia; creo que es nuestra mejor opción. Me gusta. A ver, ¿podrías conseguir el número telefónico o el nombre de esa organización? Siento que **una vez empecemos a recibir ayuda, todo cambiará**. Eso sí, planeo sacar a mi familia de ese lugar en una o dos semanas, como máximo.

Roxy: Bueno, creo que tengo el nombre en el directorio de mi teléfono celular. Dame unos segundos, a ver... ¡Aquí lo tengo! El sitio se llama *"Una segunda familia"*, y, al parecer, queda en la Calle 7 de la zona central. ¿Sabes? Al lado de la iglesia.

Vicente: ¡Ah, claro! De verdad, Roxy, **no tienes idea de cuánto me has ayudado**. ¡Qué buena amiga eres, no te imaginas! Nunca olvidaré este favor y, una vez esté en una **situación decente** nuevamente, te invitaré a cenar con tu familia a mi casa. ¡Te lo prometo!

Roxy: Está bien, ¡invitación aceptada! Eso sí, Vicente. No dependas más de las **tarjetas de crédito y los créditos bancarios. Pueden llevarte a la quiebra rápidamente**. Que sea una lección que aprendas de parte de tu amiga Roxy.

Vicente: ¡Perfecto! ¡Lo tomaré en cuenta!

English

Vicente: Damn, what am I going to do now?! This is definitely going to make things difficult.

Roxy: Hello Vicente, how are you? What's going on? I can see that **you're a bit stressed since a while ago**, and I would like to know what's making you feel that way. Is something happening right now?

Vicente: Hello Roxy, how are you doing? The truth is that **I'm not in good shape, at all**. When it comes to what's happening with me... it's quite a few things. The truth is that **things aren't going well for me**, and I've just received a **very bad news from the bank**.

Roxy: Yes? What bad news did they give you?

Vicente: They called me to tell me that had **denied a loan I requested** there a month ago, and that **they were also planning to cancel my credit card**, the same one I use monthly for **medical expenses and for groceries**. Furthermore, I recently found out **my wife is sick and that she's going to need treatment**. Now with this, none of what is coming will be easy. **It's the worst thing that's happened to me.**

Roxy: That's terrible, Vicente. I think it would be necessary to sit down and **evaluate your case**. Let's see, don't you count on family who can **get you out of trouble**, maybe with money or with medicine for your wife? There must be **someone close to you guys who can loan some money** at least, or who can contact **somebody specialized in these types of cases**.

Vicente: No, Roxy. My wife and I don't have a good relationship with our families, because they were never in agreement with our marriage, and decided to **cut ties with us**. In fact, our children don't know their grandparents, and I think that it will remain that way for a long time. The truth is that **I don't know how I'm going to maintain my household**. I have two small children!

Roxy: Well, I know someone who was in a similar situation; **she went to a charity organization**, and **they took charge of helping her out** for three months until her situation changed. **They housed her in their facilities**, gave her three meals a day, and her kids had a school transport that was

sponsored by the organization. She spent the first days upset and ashamed for being there, but finally was happy, her children were content again, and **she managed to recover and stand on her own two feet once more** as a strong woman. In your case it would be even easier because you guys are *two* adults, not just one. Don't you think?

Vicente: Well Roxy, that sounds like very good news, and I think that it's our best option. I like it. Let's see, could you find the number or the name of that organization? I feel that **once we start to receive help, everything will change**. That said, I plan to take my family out of that place within one or two weeks, maximum.

Roxy: All right, I think I have the name in the contacts of my cell phone. Give me a few seconds, let's see... Here it is! A place called *"A Second Family"*, and apparently, it's on 7th Street, Downtown. Do you know? Next to the church.

Vicente: Oh, of course! Really, Roxy, **you have no idea of how much you've helped me**. What a great friend you are, you can't imagine! I'll never forget this favor, and once I'm in a **decent situation** once more, I'll invite you to eat with your family at my place. I promise you!

Roxy: That's okay, invitation accepted! That said, Vicente. Don't depend on **credit cards and bank loans** again. **It can quickly lead you to bankruptcy**. This better be a lesson learned from your friend Roxy.

Vicente: Perfect! I'll take it into account!

CHAPTER 9

TEACHING ENTREPRENEURSHIP
LA CLASE MAGISTRAL MILLONARIA –
THE MILLIONAIRE MASTERCLASS

Vocabulary List

- **clases para emprendedores** = classes for entrepreneurs
- **anunciadas en sus redes sociales** = announced on your social media
- **preparamos empresarios** = we prepare entrepreneurs
- **ayudándolos a producir dinero** = helping them make money
- **crecer como profesionales en sus ramos** = grow as professionals in their industry
- **personas inscritas** = the people who have signed up
- **verificar** = verify
- **¿a qué te dedicas?** = what do you do for a living?
- **mi sueño es poder independizarme** = my dream is to become independent
- **no tener que depender de un empleo** = not have to depend on a job
- **escribir mis propios libros** = write my own books
- **recibir el reconocimiento que siempre he deseado** = receive the recognition that I've always wanted
- **establecer una editorial es mi sueño** = establishing a publishing company is my dream
- **tenía dudas de mis capacidades** = I had doubts about my abilities
- **miedo de dejar mi trabajo** = afraid to leave my job
- **comenzar una nueva vida de empresaria** = start a new life as an entrepreneur

- **no creía en mí misma** = I didn't believe in myself
- **dueña de una empresa de cosméticos** = owner of a cosmetics company
- **alejarme de mi trabajo formal** = walk away from my formal job
- **quiero seguir sus pasos** = I want to follow in his footsteps
- **¿alguna vez has tenido un emprendimiento?** = have you ever had a business venture?
- **siempre es bueno tener experiencia en este campo** = it's always great to have experience in this field
- **fui vendedor de golosinas importadas** = I was an imported snack salesman
- **buen negocio** = good business
- *sí* **conoces el valor del trabajo y del dinero** = you *do* know the value of work and of money
- **generar tu propio dinero** = generate your own income
- **no hay vuelta atrás** = there's no turning back
- **convertirte en emprendedor** = turn into an entrepreneur
- **empleo viejo** = old job
- **aferrado a lo viejo** = gripping onto the past
- **zona de confort** = comfort zone
- **trabajo duro** = hard work
- **hacerlo crecer como una planta** = making it grow like a plant
- **esforzarme** = making an effort
- **filosofía de vida** = life's philosophy
- **siguiente nivel en mi carrera** = the next level of my career
- **futuro emprendedor millonario** = future millionaire entrepreneur
- **una persona nueva** = a new person

Spanish

Antonio: ¡Hola! Estoy acá porque leí sobre las **clases para emprendedores**, las cuales están **anunciadas en sus redes sociales**. ¿Estoy en el lugar correcto?

Margaret: ¡Hola! ¿Qué tal? Mi nombre es Margaret y soy la directora del *Instituto para Visionarios*. Así se llama este lugar, porque **preparamos empresarios, ayudándolos a producir dinero** y **crecer como profesionales en sus ramos**. Esta es nuestra clase privada y atendemos a las **personas inscritas** a través de nuestro sistema. ¿Cuál es tu nombre? Debo **verificar**. Además, **¿a qué te dedicas** y qué deseas conseguir con esta clase?

Antonio: Oh, bueno, mi nombre es Antonio González y **mi sueño es poder independizarme** y **no tener que depender de un empleo**. Soy escritor y me encantaría **escribir mis propios libros** y **recibir el reconocimiento que siempre he deseado. Establecer una editorial es mi sueño**, una en la que pueda contratar a otros escritores que también vendan sus libros conmigo.

Margaret: Es un sueño interesante. ¿Sabes que yo también soy escritora? Alguna vez estuve en tu situación —no había publicado ningún libro, **tenía dudas de mis capacidades, miedo de dejar mi trabajo** y **comenzar una nueva vida de empresaria**, y sentía que era mejor seguir como empleada de una empresa grande—. **No creía en mí misma**, ya que no sabía que podía tener éxito haciendo las cosas por mi cuenta. ¿Tienes idea de cuánto he logrado desde que comencé a trabajar para mí misma?

Antonio: He visto un par de cosas sobre usted en las redes sociales. Es millonaria, **dueña de una empresa de cosméticos** y escritora, ¿cierto? Sueño con conseguir ese tipo de cosas, ya que mi intención es **alejarme de mi trabajo formal**. Mi padre fue un gran empresario, pero murió hace muchos años y no me dio tiempo de aprender de él. **Quiero seguir sus pasos**.

Margaret: Bueno, entonces lo mejor que pudiste haber hecho fue venir hoy para acá. **¿Alguna vez has tenido un emprendimiento?** No es necesario, pero **siempre es bueno tener experiencia en este campo**.

Antonio: Sí, de adolescente **fui vendedor de golosinas importadas**. Les vendía a mis compañeros los chocolates y dulces más ricos, traídos desde Europa y Estados Unidos. Fue un **buen negocio**, pero lo dejé de hacer una vez salí de la preparatoria.

Margaret: Es genial saberlo, entonces *sí* **conoces el valor del trabajo y del dinero**, además de que sabes que es mucho más satisfactorio **generar tu propio dinero** que depender del dinero que te paga otro, ¿cierto? Eso es lo primero que debemos tomar en cuenta. Tienes que comenzar teniendo claro que **no hay vuelta atrás** cuando decides **convertirte en emprendedor**. Hay personas que comienzan su negocio creyendo que pueden volver a su **empleo viejo**: lo dejan como un plan B y eso les daña las oportunidades de tomarse en serio su negocio.

Antonio: Vaya, sí, es cierto. A veces uno quiere comenzar algo nuevo, pero está **aferrado a lo viejo** y tiene miedo de perderlo. Creo que es la **zona de confort**.

Margaret: ¡Exacto! De eso mismo se trata: de la zona de confort y cómo tú acabas en ella. Además, a algunas personas no les gusta el **trabajo duro**, el querer despertarse cada mañana a hacer que algo funcione y luchar contra los obstáculos. *Trabajo duro,* Antonio, piensa bien en esas dos palabras. A veces somos culpables de envidiar a los que tienen dinero, pero no nos damos cuenta de todo lo que hacen a diario para poseerlo y hacerlo crecer. Se trata de cultivar el negocio, **hacerlo crecer como una planta**.

Antonio: ¡A mí me encanta trabajar duro y **esforzarme**! Es mi **filosofía de vida** y me ha funcionado bastante hasta ahora. Entonces... ¿qué es lo que necesito para llegar al **siguiente nivel en mi carrera**? ¿Qué cosas me puedes decir para prepararme como un **futuro emprendedor millonario**?

Margaret: Esa es la gran pregunta, ¿no? De eso trata esta clase, precisamente: prepararte para ser millonario. Así que llegó la hora. Concéntrate y vamos a empezar... ¡de aquí vas a salir como **una persona nueva**!

English

Antonio: Hi! I'm here because I read about the **classes for entrepreneurs,** which have been **announced on your social media**. Am I at the right place?

Margaret: Hello! How are you doing? My name is Margaret, and I'm the director at the *Institute for Visionaries*. That's the name of this place, because **we prepare entrepreneurs, helping them make money** and **grow as professionals in their industry**. This is our private class, and we serve **the people who have signed up** through our system. What is your name? I have to **verify**. Furthermore, **what do you do for a living**, and what do you hope to accomplish with this class?

Antonio: Oh, okay, my name es Antonio Gonzalez, and **my dream is to become independent** and **not have to depend on a job**. I'm a writer, and I would love to **write my own books** and **receive the recognition that I've always wanted. Establishing a publishing company is my dream**, in which I could hire other writers that would sell their own books with me.

Margaret: It's an interesting dream. Do you know I'm also a writer? I was once in your situation – I had never published a book, **I had doubts about my abilities**, I was **afraid to leave my job** and **start a new life as an entrepreneur**, and I felt that it was better to continue as the employee of a big company. **I didn't believe in myself**, since I wasn't aware I could be successful doing things on my own. Do you have any idea how much I've accomplished since I started to work for myself?

Antonio: I've seen a few things about you on social media. You're a millionaire, **owner of a cosmetics company** and a writer, right? I dream with accomplishing that type of thing, since my intention is to **walk away from my formal job**. My father was a great businessman, but he died many years ago and I wasn't able to learn from him. **I want to follow in his footsteps**.

Margaret: Well, then the best thing you could have done was coming here today. **Have you ever had a business venture?** It's not necessary, but **it's always great to have experience in this field**.

Antonio: Yes, as a teenager **I was an imported snack salesman**. I sold the most delicious chocolates and sweets from Europe and the United States to my classmates. It was a **good business**, but I stopped doing it once I left high school.

Margaret: That's great to know, so **you *do* know the value of work and of money**, as well as knowing that it's much more satisfying to **generate your own income** than depending on the money paid by somebody else, right? That's the first thing we have to take into account. You have to start by being clear in that **there's no turning back** when you decide to **turn into an entrepreneur**. There are people who start their business thinking that they can return to their **old job**: they leave it there as a plan B, and that damages their opportunities of taking their business seriously.

Antonio: Wow, yeah, that's right. Sometimes, one wants to start something new, but you're **gripping onto the past** and afraid to lose it. I think it's the **comfort zone**.

Margaret: Exactly! That's precisely what it's about: the comfort zone, and how you end up in it. Furthermore, some people don't like **hard work**, wanting to wake up every day to do something that works and to fight against obstacles. *Hard work,* Antonio, think hard on these two words. Sometimes we're guilty of envying those with money, but we don't realize everything they do every day to have it and make it grow. It's about nurturing the business, **making it grow like a plant**.

Antonio: I love working hard and **making an effort**! It's my **life's philosophy,** and it has served me well until now. So... what do I need to get to **the next level of my career**? What things can you tell me to prepare me as a **future millionaire entrepreneur**?

Margaret: That's the great question, isn't it? That's what this class is about, precisely – preparing you to become a millionaire. So the time has come. Concentrate and let's begin... you're going to walk out of here as **a new person**!

CHAPTER 10

OPENING A BANK ACCOUNT
CUMPLIENDO CON LOS REQUISITOS – FULFILLING THE REQUIREMENTS

Vocabulary List

- **donde ayudamos a construir sueños** = where we help to build dreams
- **¿en qué le puedo servir?** = in what may I serve you?
- **quisiera crear una cuenta bancaria en esta sucursal** = I would like to create a bank account at this branch
- **¿qué tipo de cuenta va a querer?** = what type of account do you wish to open?
- **¿qué tipo de cuentas ofrece?** = what type of accounts does this bank offer?
- **cuenta de banco tipo corriente** = current bank account
- **chequera** = checkbook
- **un alto límite de transferencias y retiros mensuales** = a high monthly limit of transfers and withdrawals
- **la posibilidad de solicitar créditos** = possibility of requesting loans
- **dentro de los primeros cuatro meses de haber creado su cuenta** = within the first four months of having created the account
- **poder guardar su dinero en un lugar seguro** = saving your money in a safe place
- **la cuenta de ahorros** = savings account
- **tenga su dinero en nuestras bóvedas generándole intereses** = saving your cash in our vaults while generating interests
- **su dinero crecerá mientras usted está tranquilo** = your money will grow while you're relaxed
- **una cuenta juvenil para los más pequeños de la casa** = a junior

account for the little ones at home

- **¿qué requisitos voy a necesitar para esto?** = what requirements do I need for this?
- **necesitará traer una copia de su documento de identidad** = you will need to bring a copy of your identity document
- **una carta de trabajo o título de empresa** = an employment letter or company ownership letter
- **tres recibos de pago recientes** = three recent payslips
- **prueba de domicilio** = a proof of domicile
- **un recibo a su nombre** = a utilities bill in your name
- **dos referencias personales** = two personal references
- **un depósito inicial** = an initial deposit
- **pronto podrá disfrutar de los servicios que ofrecemos en persona y en línea** = soon you'll be able to enjoy the services we offer in person and online
- **proceso de apertura** = opening process
- **verificar los documentos e introducir su información** = verify the documents and input your information
- **tarjeta de débito** = debit card
- **tarjeta de crédito** = credit card
- **una contraseña** = password
- **comenzar a usarla en sus establecimientos favoritos** = start using it in your favorite establishments
- **fue un placer ser atendido por usted** = it was a pleasure to be served by you

Spanish

Daniela: Buen día, señor. Bienvenido al Banco Unido, **donde ayudamos a construir sueños. ¿En qué le puedo servir?**

Pedro: Buenos días, señorita. Estoy aquí el día de hoy porque **quisiera crear una cuenta bancaria en esta sucursal.** ¿Es posible hacerlo?

Daniela: Por supuesto que sí, señor. Lo primero que le voy a preguntar es: **¿qué tipo de cuenta va a querer?**

Pedro: No había pensado en eso. A ver, **¿qué tipo de cuentas ofrece** Banco Unido?

Daniela: Bueno, en primer lugar, tenemos una **cuenta de banco tipo corriente,** la cual incluye una **chequera, un alto límite de transferencias y retiros mensuales, y la posibilidad de solicitar créditos dentro de los primeros cuatro meses de haber creado su cuenta.** Esta es la más común, y puede servirle a todos nuestros clientes, sin importar su condición.

Pedro: Interesante, suena bien. ¿Qué otro tipo de cuenta puedo crear el día de hoy?

Daniela: Si no es fanático de los altos límites y lo que desea, más bien, es **poder guardar su dinero en un lugar seguro,** tenemos **la cuenta de ahorros,** la cual sirve para que usted **tenga su dinero en nuestras bóvedas generándole intereses.** Así, **su dinero crecerá mientras usted está tranquilo.** ¿Es esta su cuenta preferida?

Pedro: Puede ser, pero quisiera saber si aún sigue habiendo otros tipos de cuenta en su banco.

Daniela: Por ser un cliente nuevo, solo puedo ofrecerle estos dos tipos de cuenta de banco. Además, tenemos **una cuenta juvenil para los más pequeños de la casa,** que permite a los jóvenes menores de dieciséis años abrir una cuenta en nuestra sucursal, si está interesado en abrir una cuenta a sus hijos u otros familiares.

Pedro: Suena bien, pero entonces voy a querer una cuenta corriente. **¿Qué requisitos voy a necesitar para esto?**

Daniela: Muy buena elección, señor. Para abrir una cuenta corriente en Banco Unido **necesitará traer una copia de su documento de identidad,**

una carta de trabajo o título de empresa, tres recibos de pago recientes, prueba de domicilio, un recibo a su nombre y dos referencias personales. Con esto, y **un depósito inicial**, podremos abrir una cuenta y pronto podrá disfrutar de los servicios que ofrecemos en persona y en línea. ¿Qué piensa de esto?

Pedro: Me parece excelente, tengo buen tiempo queriendo abrir una cuenta y no suena como que los requisitos son difíciles de conseguir... de hecho, creo que puedo venir en una hora y traerle eso. ¿Estará aquí en una hora para culminar el **proceso de apertura** de la cuenta corriente?

Daniela: Sí, estaré esperándolo entonces para servirle.

Una hora después...

Pedro: De acuerdo, aquí tengo todos los requisitos, además de cien dólares que pienso usar para habilitar la cuenta.

Daniela: Excelente, permítame unos minutos para **verificar los documentos e introducir su información** al sistema. De acuerdo, aquí tiene sus documentos de vuelta, ya estoy realizando la apertura de la cuenta. En un momento le entregaré su **tarjeta de débito** y su chequera. Podrá solicitar una **tarjeta de crédito** dentro de quince días. ¿Está bien?

Pedro: Es una excelente noticia, no veo la hora de comenzar a usar mis tarjetas de débito y crédito.

Daniela: Bien, aquí tiene su tarjeta, debe firmar que la ha recibido aquí, aquí y aquí. Ahora firme acá para confirmar la recepción de su chequera. Perfecto, señor Pedro López... ¡ya es cliente del Banco Unido! Felicitaciones, ya puede establecer **una contraseña** para su tarjeta de débito y **comenzar a usarla en sus establecimientos favoritos**. ¿Puedo servirle en algo más?

Pedro: No, gracias. Fue todo, muchísimas gracias, señorita Daniela. **Fue un placer ser atendido por usted.**

Daniela: No hay problema, que tenga mucha suerte; ¡gracias por utilizar Banco Unido!

English

Daniela: Good day, sir. Welcome to United Bank, **where we help to build dreams. In what may I serve you?**

Pedro: Good morning, young lady. I'm here today because **I would like to create a bank account at this branch.** Is it possible to do that?

Daniela: Of course it is, sir. The first thing I'm going to ask is – **what type of account do you wish to open?**

Pedro: I hadn't thought of that. Let's see, **what type of accounts does United Bank offer?**

Daniela: Well, firstly we have the **current bank account,** which includes a **checkbook, a high monthly limit of transfers and withdrawals,** as well as the **possibility of requesting loans within the first four months of having created the account.** This is the most common account, and it can serve all of our clients, regardless of their condition.

Pedro: Interesting, sounds good. What other type of account can I create today?

Daniela: If you're not a fan of high limits and you prefer **saving your money in a safe place** instead, we have our **savings account,** which serves you in **saving your cash in our vaults while generating interests.** That way, **your money will grow while you're relaxed.** Is this your preferred account?

Pedro: Perhaps, but I would like to know if there are still other types of accounts in this bank.

Daniela: Since you're a new client, I can only offer these two types of bank account. Furthermore, we have **a junior account for the little ones at home,** which allows young people of under sixteen years of age to open an account at our branch, if you're interested in opening an account for your children or other family members.

Pedro: Sounds good, but I'm actually going to want a current account. **What requirements do I need for this?**

Daniela: Very good choice, sir. To open a current account at United Bank, **you will need to bring a copy of your identity document, an employment**

letter or company ownership letter, three recent payslips, a proof of domicile, a utilities bill in your name and **two personal references**. With this, as well as **an initial deposit**, we'll be able to open an account and **soon you'll be able to enjoy the services we offer in person and online**. What do you think about this?

Pedro: I think it's great, I've been wanting to open an account for a while and it doesn't sound like the requirements are hard to obtain... actually, I think I can come back in an hour and bring that with me. Will you be here in an hour so we can finish the **opening process** for the current account?

Daniela: Yes, I will be waiting to serve you, then.

One hour later...

Pedro: Very well, I have all the requirements here, as well as one hundred dollars that I wish to use to enable the account.

Daniela: Excellent, allow me a few minutes to **verify the documents and input your information** onto the system. Very well, here you can have your documents back, I'm opening your account now. In a moment, I'll hand you your **debit card** and your checkbook. You'll be able to request a **credit card** within fifteen days. Is that okay?

Pedro: It's excellent news, I can't wait to start using my debit and credit cards.

Daniela: Great, here's your card, you must sign here, here and here to prove you've received it. Now sign here to prove you've received your checkbook. Perfect, Mr. Pedro Lopez... you're now a client of United Bank! Congratulations, you can now set **a password** for your debit card and **start using it in your favorite establishments**. Can I serve you in anything else?

Pedro: No, thanks. That was everything, thanks a lot, Miss Daniela. **It was a pleasure to be served by you**.

Daniela: There's no problem, I wish you good luck; thank you for using United Bank!

CHAPTER 11

MAKING A SALE
CÓMPRALO HOY O TE ARREPENTIRÁS –
BUY IT TODAY OR YOU'LL REGRET IT

Vocabulary List

- **quiero vender unas cosas de mi casa que ya no usamos** = I want to sell some things from home that we no longer use
- **quería ver si alguien estaba interesado o interesada en ellas** = I wanted to know if somebody was interested in them
- **todas están en buenas condiciones** = everything is in good condition
- **me acabo de mudar** = I just moved
- **tengo muy pocos aparatos electrónicos y adornos** = I have very few electrical appliances and decorations
- **déjame ver qué estás vendiendo** = let me see what you're selling
- **gracias por tu interés** = thanks for your interest
- **aquí está todo lo que estoy vendiendo** = here is everything that I'm selling
- **prendas de lencería para el hogar** = linen garments for your home
- **un batidor para preparar postres** = a mixer to prepare dessert
- **pasteles y dulces** = cakes and sweets
- **sus golosinas favoritas** = their favorite snacks
- **aquí tengo una opción perfecta para ti** = I have a perfect option for you right here
- **es de buena marca** = it's of a good brand
- **es excelente, súper recomendado** = it's excellent, super recommended

- **me lo llevaré entonces** = I'll take it with me then
- **puedes tocarlas y ver su calidad** = you can touch them and see their quality
- **me las llevo todas** = I'll take them all
- **bajo consumo eléctrico** = low electrical consumption
- **te lo recomiendo** = I recommend it
- **está en buenas condiciones** = it's in good condition
- **¿alguna otra cosa que desees saber o ver?** = anything else you want to know or see?
- **¿quieres que haga una transferencia, o te lo pago en efectivo?** = do you want me to make a transfer or should I pay you in cash?
- **recuerda decirle a tus compañeras y amigas que tengo todo esto** = remember to tell your fellow workers and friends that I have all this
- **¡necesito venderlo todo!** = I need to sell it all!

Spanish

James: ¡Hola, chicos! Disculpen por hacer esto en la oficina, pero **quiero vender unas cosas de mi casa que ya no usamos** y quería ver si alguien estaba interesado o interesada en ellas. Todas están en buenas condiciones, así que puede que se vendan en su totalidad. ¿Alguien que quiera ver? ¿No?

Fernanda: Yo estoy interesada, James. **Me acabo de mudar** y me hacen falta unas cuantas cosas en mi nuevo apartamento; **tengo muy pocos aparatos electrónicos y adornos**, y la verdad es que se ve vacío. **Déjame ver qué estás vendiendo.**

James: Excelente, Fernanda. **Gracias por tu interés.** Sígueme a mi oficina. Bueno, como verás, **aquí está todo lo que estoy vendiendo.** En esta esquina de la oficina tengo los aparatos electrónicos; en este lado están los adornos. También tengo **prendas de lencería para el hogar**, las cuales te servirán si estás comenzando una nueva vida.

Fernanda: Bueno, comencemos. Necesito **un batidor para preparar postres** para mis hijos, lo cierto es que ellos aman comer **pasteles y dulces**, y no pienso dejarlos sin disfrutar de **sus golosinas favoritas** solo porque nos mudamos.

James: ¡Excelente! En ese caso, **aquí tengo una opción perfecta para ti**: solo la usé durante unos meses para preparar wafles y, además, ha estado en su caja desde la primera y última vez que fue usada. **Es de buena marca** y tiene control de velocidades. Además, tiene varios cabezales para que puedas controlar cómo vas a batir los líquidos para tus pasteles. **Es excelente, súper recomendado.**

Fernanda: Genial, **me lo llevaré entonces.** Ponlo allí. Ahora, necesito varias toallas, ya que actualmente mis hijos y yo solo tenemos una toalla cada uno. Eso no es muy higiénico que digamos, ¿cierto?

James: No, para nada. En este caso, tengo unas toallas importadas, hechas de algodón egipcio, de colores variados y muy hermosas. Están limpias, **puedes tocarlas y ver su calidad.** ¿Ya ves? Tengo para la cara y el cuerpo, y, si las compras todas, tengo un descuento para ti. Son ocho en total.

Fernanda: ¡Me gusta cómo suena eso! Sí, **me las llevo todas**. Oye, ¿es esto lo que pienso que es? ¿Una plancha de cabello?

James: Sí, es precisamente eso. Tiene un buen rango de temperaturas, además de un sensor que hace cambiar automáticamente la temperatura si tu cabello está recibiendo demasiado calor. Es de **bajo consumo eléctrico** y puede ser usado sin conectar, por varios minutos, con una batería recargable. **Te lo recomiendo** —mi esposa lo usaba para ocasiones especiales, pero luego comenzó a ir más a la peluquería—.

Fernanda: Sí, bueno, déjame considerarlo y te respondo cuando haya visto lo demás. Cuéntame, ¿tienes artículos para bebés? Ya sabes que tengo un niño de un año y se me ha vuelto cuesta arriba conseguir todos los accesorios que eso conlleva. Si tienes el asiento de bebé para autos, por ejemplo...

James: Eso no lo traje conmigo hoy, pero sí, en efecto, lo tengo. **Está en buenas condiciones**, ya que lo usábamos con cuidado y lo tengo envuelto en plástico en casa. Mañana te lo podría traer y lo ves. Bueno, **¿alguna otra cosa que desees saber o ver?** Tengo mucho más, solo que no pude traerlo todo a la oficina.

Fernanda: Creo que, por ahora, vamos con esto, ya que tampoco quiero descompletar el salario. **¿Quieres que haga una transferencia, o te lo pago en efectivo?**

James: Una transferencia me sirve. **Recuerda decirle a tus compañeras y amigas que tengo todo esto, ¡necesito venderlo todo!**

Fernanda: Seguro, ¡lo haré!

English

James: Hey guys! Sorry for doing this at the office, but **I want to sell some things from home that we no longer use**, and **I wanted to know if somebody was interested in them.** Everything is in good condition, so it's possible for me to sell absolutely everything. Anyone that wants to check it out? No?

Fernanda: I'm interested, James. **I just moved**, and I need quite a few things at our new apartment; **I have very few electrical appliances and decorations**, and the truth is that it looks empty. **Let me see what you're selling**.

James: Excellent, Fernanda. **Thanks for your interest.** Follow me to my office. Anyway, as you can see, **here is everything that I'm selling.** In this corner of the office I have the electrical appliances; on this side are the decorations. I also have **linen garments for your home**, which will serve you if you're starting off a new life.

Fernanda: Well, let's begin. I need **a mixer to prepare dessert** for my kids, the truth is that they love to eat **cakes and sweets**, and I don't think I'm going to let them be without enjoying **their favorite snacks** just because we've moved.

James: Excellent! In that case **I have a perfect option for you right here:** I only used it for a few months to prepare waffles, and it's also been inside its box since the first and last time it was used. **It's of a good brand**, and it has a speed control. Furthermore, it includes several tips so that you can control how you're going to mix the liquids for your cakes. **It's excellent, super recommended**.

Fernanda: Great, **I'll take it with me then**. Put it there. Now, I need several towels, since right now my kids and I only have one towel each. That's not very hygienic if you think about it, right?

James: Nope, not at all. In this case, I have imported towels, made from Egyptian cotton, beautiful and of varied colors. They're clean, **you can touch them and see their quality.** Can you see? I have towels for both face and body, and if you buy them all, I have a discount for you. There are eight in total.

Fernanda: I love how that sounds! Yeah, **I'll take them all.** Hey, is this what I think it is? A flat iron?

James: Yeah, it's precisely that. It has a good range of temperatures, as well as a sensor which automatically changes the temperature if your hair is receiving too much heat. It's of **low electrical consumption** and can be used without connecting for several minutes with a rechargeable battery. **I recommend it** – my wife used it for special occasions, but then she started to visit the hairdresser more often.

Fernanda: Yeah, sure, let me consider it and I'll answer when I've seen the rest. Tell me now, do you have items for babies? You know I have a boy of one year, and it has become tough to find all of the accessories that he needs. If you have an infant car seat, for example...

James: I didn't bring that with me today, but yeah, I definitely have it. **It's in good condition**, since we used it with care and I have it wrapped in plastic at home. Tomorrow I could bring it to you, and you check it out. Okay, **anything else you want to know or see?** I have a lot more; I just couldn't bring it all to the office.

Fernanda: I think that for now let's go forward with this, since I don't want to wreak havoc on my wages. **Do you want me to make a transfer or should I pay you in cash?**

James: A transfer is okay. **Remember to tell your fellow workers and friends that I have all this, I need to sell it all!**

Fernanda: Sure, will do!

CHAPTER 12

CONVINCING THE BOARD
EL SISTEMA DE SEGURIDAD –
THE SECURITY SYSTEM

Vocabulary List

- **supervisor de la División de Tecnología de Información y Comunicación** = supervisor of the company's communication and information technology division
- **gracias por asistir a mi presentación** = giving you my thanks for coming to my presentation
- **sugerencias de mejoras** = suggestions on improvements
- **sistema de seguridad digital de la empresa** = the company's digital security system
- **directiva de la empresa** = company's board of directors
- **presidente y cofundadora de esta empresa** = president and co-founder of this company
- **hablaré en nombre de mis compañeros** = I will speak in the name of my fellow board members
- **te doy el derecho de palabra** = I'll give you the right to speak
- **¿de qué trata esta presentación y qué propuestas traes?** = what is this presentation about and what proposals do you bring?
- **desempeño del personal de seguridad** = the performance of the security staff
- **las fallas que llevaron a pérdidas** = the breaches that led to losses
- **el acceso a las altas esferas de información** = the access to the higher spheres of information
- **personas no autorizadas** = non-authorized staff
- **método adicional de seguridad** = an additional method of

security
- **fugas de información** = information leaks
- **sistema de múltiples capas de cifrado** = system of multiple layers of encryption
- **acceso a cada nivel de información** = access the information located behind each level
- **verificar su identidad** = verify your identity
- **¿de cuánto estamos hablando en cuanto a inversión?** = how much are we talking about in terms of investment?
- **Departamento de Tecnología de Información** = Department of information technology
- **universidad prestigiosa** = prestigious university
- **propuestas de pasantías y trabajos de grado** = internship and thesis work proposals
- **colaboración no muy significativa** = not very significant donation
- **pequeña inversión en dinero y en asesorías** = small investment in money and in consulting
- **¿por cuánto tiempo tendríamos el sistema funcionando?** = for how long would we have this system working?
- **¿cuánto tiempo tardaría en instalarse?** = how long would it take to install it?
- **una vez se venza la licencia** = once the new one's license runs out
- **renovable** = renewable
- **podremos contar con asistencia técnica** = we would count on technical assistance
- **habiendo discutido esto con mis compañeros** = having discussed this with my fellow board members
- **el veredicto es el siguiente** = the verdict is the following
- **sí, queremos aprobar este proyecto** = yes, we want to approve this project
- **incluir otros beneficios y funciones de este sistema** = include other benefits and functions of this system
- **hoy has conseguido un gran logro** = today you have accomplished a great achievement

- **los procesos de inscripción y contratación** = the sign-up and contract processes

Spanish

Ronald: Hola a todos y bienvenidos. Mi nombre es Ronald Miller y soy **supervisor de la División de Tecnología de Información y Comunicación** en la empresa. Quiero comenzar por darles las **gracias por asistir a mi presentación** sobre las **sugerencias de mejoras** en el **sistema de seguridad digital de la empresa** y pedirles que presten atención a lo que viene.

Sally: Buen día, Ronald. Aquí estamos todos los de la **directiva de la empresa**. Ya debes saber quién soy, pero, por si no lo sabes, soy Sally Smith, **presidenta y cofundadora de esta empresa**. El día de hoy **hablaré en nombre de mis compañeros**, pero si alguien más desea contribuir, puede hacerlo. Ahora, **te doy el derecho de palabra**... cuéntanos, **¿de qué trata esta presentación y qué propuestas traes?**

Ronald: De acuerdo, comenzaré preguntándoles brevemente sobre los resultados de este año, que acaba de culminar, con respecto a la seguridad de la empresa. ¿Están contentos con el **desempeño del personal de seguridad**? ¿Notaron **las fallas que llevaron a pérdidas** en, al menos, tres incidentes durante febrero, junio y noviembre?

Sally: La verdad es que, si debo ser sincera, no estoy contenta con el desempeño de este personal. Realmente pienso que **el acceso a las altas esferas de información** en nuestros registros debería estar mejor protegida y mucho menos accesible para **personas no autorizadas**. Sí notamos las fallas, ya que estas implicaron pérdidas casi millonarias, y debemos establecer un **método adicional de seguridad** para evitar **fugas de información**.

Ronald: Exactamente. Estoy de acuerdo con usted, y es por eso que he seleccionado un **sistema de múltiples capas de cifrado** para el **acceso a cada nivel de información**. De hecho, incluso ustedes aquí presentes, tendrían que **verificar su identidad** con múltiples métodos para acceder a la información que se ubicará detrás de cada capa de cifrado. Sería un sistema de verificación que no posee actualmente ninguna empresa de la competencia y que únicamente se ha visto implementado en cinco de las empresas más grandes del mundo. Aquí puede visualizar un poco como funciona.

Sally: Es interesante esta propuesta, ciertamente... pero **¿de cuánto estamos hablando en cuanto a inversión?** Suena como algo costoso que podría no ser factible para implementar.

Ronald: Esa es la mejor parte. Gracias a un acuerdo entre mi persona y el **Departamento de Tecnología de Información** de una **universidad prestigiosa**, entre las cinco mejores de EE. UU., podremos recibir estos sistemas de seguridad a cambio de **propuestas de pasantías y trabajos de grado** para los estudiantes de dicha universidad, además de una **colaboración no muy significativa.** Es decir, con una **pequeña inversión en dinero y en asesorías**, podríamos poseer un sistema que protegería nuestra información como casi ninguno en el mundo. Y ya saben, la información es conocimiento, y el conocimiento es poder.

Sally: Eso suena genial. ¿Cuándo hiciste contacto con ese departamento de la universidad? Sería interesante hacer otras propuestas, pero, por ahora, esta me gusta mucho. Ahora, **¿por cuánto tiempo tendríamos el sistema funcionando** y **cuánto tiempo tardaría en instalarse?** Me preocupa que luego tendremos que regresar al problemático sistema actual **una vez se venza la licencia** y se hayan ido los pasantes de la universidad. ¿Cómo lidiamos con esto?

Ronald: Buena pregunta, y no, no se vencerá de tal manera. La propuesta de la universidad es que el trato dure cinco años, sin más condiciones que las que nombré. Tendremos una licencia de cinco años, **renovable** si lo acordamos así, y **podremos contar con asistencia técnica** de sus creadores hasta el final del acuerdo. Esto es perfecto, ya que no todos necesitaremos aprender a usarlo o repararlo en tal caso. ¿Qué opina de esto? Yo pienso que es una genial idea seguir adelante con este sistema, pero todo depende de ustedes, el comité.

Sally: Bueno, **habiendo discutido esto con mis compañeros, el veredicto es el siguiente: sí, queremos aprobar este proyecto**, y pronto abriremos plazas para que puedan empezar a ingresar pasantes de la universidad a nuestros departamentos. Espero que puedas renovar tu presentación e **incluir otros beneficios y funciones de este sistema**, pero definitivamente vamos a aprobar esta propuesta. Gracias, Ronald, **hoy has conseguido un gran logro.**

Ronald: ¡Excelente, presidenta! Hoy mismo comenzaré a contactar a los involucrados para llevar a cabo **los procesos de inscripción y**

contratación. ¡Gracias a todos por su atención!

English

Ronald: Hello everyone, and welcome. My name is Ronald Miller, and I'm a **supervisor** of the **company's communication and information technology division**. I want to begin by **giving you my thanks for coming to my presentation** about the **suggestions on improvements** for the **company's digital security system**, and request that you pay attention to what's coming next.

Sally: Good day, Ronald. Everybody within the **company's board of directors** is here. You should know who I am, but if you don't, I'm Sally Smith, **president and co-founder of this company**. Today **I will speak in the name of my fellow board members**, but if anyone else wants to contribute, they can do so. Now, **I'll give you the right to speak**... tell us, **what is this presentation about and what proposals do you bring?**

Ronald: All right, let's start with asking you about this last year's results in terms of the company's security. Are you content with **the performance of the security staff**? Did you note **the breaches that led to losses** in at least three incidents during February, June and November?

Sally: The truth is that I must be honest, and I'm not happy with the performance of this staff. I truly think that **the access to the higher spheres of information** in our registries should be better protected and much less accessible to **non-authorized staff**. We did note the breaches, since these led to almost million-dollar losses, and we must establish **an additional method of security** to prevent **information leaks**.

Ronald: Exactly. I'm in agreement with you, and that is why I've selected a **system of multiple layers of encryption** for the access to each level of information. In fact, even you who are present today would have to **verify your identity** with several methods to **access the information located behind each level** of encryption. It would be a verification system that no company in the competition possesses, and which has only been implemented in five of the biggest companies of the world. Here you can briefly visualize how it works.

Sally: The proposition is interesting, but... **how much are we talking about in terms of investment?** It sounds like something expensive that might not be feasible to put in place.

Ronald: That's the best part. Thanks to an agreement between myself and the **department of information technology** at a **prestigious university** within the top five in the U.S., we could receive these security systems in exchange for **internship and thesis work proposals,** as well as a **not very significant donation.** In other words, with a **small investment in money and in consulting,** we could possess a system that would protect our information almost like none in the world. And you already know, information is knowledge, and knowledge is power.

Sally: That sounds great – when did you make contact with that department of the university? It would be interesting to make more proposals, but for now this one is one I like a lot. Now, **for how long would we have this system working,** and **how long would it take to install it?** I'm worried that we'd then have to return to the current, troublesome system **once the new one's license runs out** and the university interns have left. How do we deal with that?

Ronald: Good question, and no, it won't run out like that. The proposition of the university is that the deal last for five years, without more conditions than the ones I named. We would have a five-year license, **renewable** if we agree it that way, and **we would count on technical assistance** from its creators until the end of the deal. That is perfect, since not all of us would need to learn to use or repair it in such a case. What is your opinion on this? I think that it's a great idea to go forward with this system, but it all depends on you, the board.

Sally: Well, **having discussed this with my fellow board members, the verdict is the following: yes, we want to approve this project,** and soon we will open vacancies to allow the entry of university interns to our departments. I hope you can renew your presentation and **include other benefits and functions of this system,** but we'll definitely approve this proposal. Thank you, Ronald, **today you have accomplished a great achievement.**

Ronald: Excellent, president! From today I'll start contacting the people involved to begin **the sign-up and contract processes.** Thanks to everybody for your attention!

CHAPTER 13

PERSONNEL TRAINING
ASÍ ES COMO LO HACES – THIS IS HOW YOU DO IT

Vocabulary List

- **capacitación anual de personal** = yearly personnel training
- **supervisora de personal** = personnel supervisor
- **entrenamiento** = training
- **aprendizajes importantes** = important lessons
- **gerencia efectiva de personal** = effective management of staff
- **suministrado** = provided
- **grabada** = filmed
- **tendrás acceso** = you will have access
- **procesos de capacitación anteriores** = previous training processes
- **personalizadas** = customized
- **tengo poco trato con los clientes** = I deal little with clients
- **producción de contenido para publicidad y mercadeo** = production of content for advertising and marketing
- **director creativo** = creative director
- **empatizar más** = empathize more
- **sin necesidad de que tu gerente intervenga** = without needing your manager to intervene
- **te abriría más campo en la empresa** = open more opportunities for you within the company
- **comportamiento adecuado para esta situación** = the right behavior for this situation
- **organizar y dirigir** = organize and direct
- **llevar a un grupo de personas a una meta** = lead a group of people to a goal

- **las personas no necesitan estar por debajo del líder** = people don't need to be below a leader
- **estar al mismo nivel** = be at the same level
- **el líder toma las riendas y los ayuda a encontrar su propósito** = the leader grabs the reins and helps them find their purpose
- **estatus** = status
- **llega hasta la solución** = arrives at a solution
- **algo a lo que debes aspirar** = something that you must aspire to
- **no dejar que la vida te pase de largo** = not allow life to pass you by
- **el poder de gerenciar** = the power of management
- **entorno laboral** = working environment
- **los mejores líderes y gerentes** = the best leaders and managers
- **trabajadores más humildes** = the humblest workers
- **el estrato más bajo** = the lowest tier
- **un simple empleado** = a simple employee
- **¡excelente análisis!** = excellent analysis!
- **no tienen ni la menor idea** = don't have the faintest idea
- **cómo lograr el cambio** = how to make a change
- **trabajar en convertirme en un mejor líder** = working on transforming me into a better leader

Spanish

Patricia: ¡Bienvenido a la **capacitación anual de personal**, Hernán Rivas! Soy Patricia Núñez, **supervisora de personal.** Como ya habrás sido informado previamente, en este **entrenamiento** recibirás **aprendizajes importantes** sobre la atención al cliente, el liderazgo y la **gerencia efectiva de personal.** ¿Tienes alguna pregunta antes de que comencemos o estamos listos?

Hernán: Buen día, Patricia. Sí, solo una pregunta. ¿Dónde debo tomar nota para esta clase? No fui **suministrado** con un bolígrafo o papel para esto.

Patricia: No harán falta, ¡tranquilo! Esta clase será **grabada** y **tendrás acceso** a ella más adelante, a través de tu cuenta de la empresa. Ahora, comencemos con una pregunta de mi parte. ¿Qué tal te ha ido con los **procesos de capacitación anteriores?**

Hernán: Me ha ido regular, la verdad. Anteriormente no eran **personalizadas**, sino que era un instructor ante cien estudiantes. Era un poco difícil recibir la atención merecida. Esta vez, creo que aprenderé más.

Patricia: Sí, me aseguraré de eso. A ver, ¿qué experiencia tienes con la atención al cliente en tu cargo?

Hernán: Para ser sincero, **tengo poco trato con los clientes**, ya que mi trabajo se trata más sobre la **producción de contenido para publicidad y mercadeo.** No entro directamente en contacto con los clientes, sino más bien mi jefe, el **director creativo.**

Patricia: Entiendo. Pero... ¿sabías que las habilidades de atención al cliente te permiten **empatizar más** con esas personas a las cuales les estás produciendo esos contenidos? Y, además, ¿qué quizás te permitiría entrar en contacto directo con el cliente, **sin necesidad de que tu gerente intervenga?** Esto **te abriría más campo en la empresa** y, ¿quién sabe?, podrías acabar trabajando al lado del director creativo, como su asistente.

Hernán: Vaya, es cierto. Sí me serviría de mucho aprender sobre la atención al cliente. ¿Por dónde debo comenzar?

Patricia: Todo tiene que iniciar con el correcto saludo y el **comportamiento adecuado para esta situación**. No todos los clientes son iguales, ni tampoco lo son las situaciones que se presentarán. En esto entra el liderazgo, el cual mencioné anteriormente. Antes de continuar, te pregunto: ¿qué sabes sobre el liderazgo y qué es para ti un líder?

Hernán: El liderazgo es la capacidad de una persona de **organizar y dirigir** a otras que están por debajo de él o ella, ¿cierto? Un líder es la persona que toma este rol y lo usa para **llevar a un grupo de personas a una meta.**

Patricia: Tu respuesta es bastante acertada, pero hay algo que no es necesariamente cierto —**las personas no necesitan estar** *por debajo* del **líder**; pueden **estar al mismo nivel**, solo que **el líder toma las riendas y los ayuda a encontrar su propósito**—. De hecho, un buen líder verdadero no mira a las personas por su **estatus**, sino que se organiza junto a todos y **llega hasta la solución.** Es **algo a lo que debes aspirar**, Hernán, y **no dejar que la vida te pase de largo** mientras te decides en lo que realmente deseas.

Hernán: Sí, estoy de acuerdo. Ahora, el otro tema del cual íbamos a hablar era el de la **gerencia efectiva de personal**. ¿Sobre qué trata esto? Como ya mencioné, no soy gerente ni tengo a alguien bajo mi cargo.

Patricia: El poder de gerenciar es como el liderazgo: no importa en qué nivel estás, igual puedes aprender y lograr grandes cosas en tu **entorno laboral**. De hecho, un estudio dice que **los mejores líderes y gerentes** salen de los **trabajadores más humildes** que alguna vez estuvieron en **el estrato más bajo** de las empresas. Y, ¿sabes por qué ocurre esto?

Hernán: A ver, ¿será porque les ha tocado ver las necesidades y los problemas por los que pasa **un simple empleado**, cosa que no les sucede a los empleados que comienzan desde más arriba?

Patricia: ¡Excelente análisis! Es justamente eso. Saben que las personas que llegan asignadas a puestos de gerente tienen ciertos problemas de ego, y muchas veces **no tienen ni la menor idea** de cómo vive el trabajador o de qué sobrevive. Es por esto que las personas que ya han vivido esas dificultades tienen una alta posibilidad de llenar estos puestos, en vista de que van a saber trabajar mejor con los trabajadores de bajos estratos.

Hernán: Es increíblemente valiosa la información que me estás proporcionando, Patricia, ¡de verdad! Y aún no comenzamos el entrenamiento, ¿cierto?

Patricia: Así es. Apenas vamos a comenzar. Por eso debes seguir prestando atención. Te voy a hablar del porqué, **cómo lograr el cambio,** qué casos reales se han presentado y, además, darte una oportunidad de trabajo que te va a encantar.

Hernán: ¡Suena fascinante! ¡Vamos, entonces! ¡Comencemos a **trabajar en convertirme en un mejor líder!**

English

Patricia: Welcome to the **yearly personnel training**, Hernan Rivas! I'm Patricia Nuñez, **personnel supervisor**. As you may have already been informed, in this **training**, you will receive **important lessons** about customer service, leadership and the **effective management of staff**. Do you have any questions before we begin or are we ready?

Hernan: Good morning, Patricia. Yes, it was just one question. Where can I take notes for this class? I wasn't **provided** with a pen or a pencil for this.

Patricia: They won't be necessary, don't worry! This class will be **filmed**, and **you will have access** to it further ahead through your company account. Now, let's begin with a question of my own. How has it gone for you in **previous training processes**?

Hernan: It's been so-so, to be honest. Previously, they weren't **customized**, instead it was one instructor standing before one hundred students. It was quite difficult to receive the deserved attention. This time, I think I'll learn more.

Patricia: Yeah, I'll make sure of that. Let's see, what experience do you have with customer service in your position?

Hernan: Sincerely, **I deal little with clients**, since my work is mainly about the **production of content for advertising and marketing**. I don't actually come directly into contact with the customers, which is actually the role of my boss, the **creative director**.

Patricia: I understand. But... did you know that the skills involving customer service allow you to **empathize more** with the people who you're producing that content for? And also, that perhaps it could allow you to enter in direct contact with a customer **without needing your manager to intervene**? This would **open more opportunities for you within the company**, and who knows? You could end up working alongside the creative director as his assistant.

Hernan: Wow, that's true. It would help me a lot to learn about customer service. Where must I begin?

Patricia: Everything has to start with the correct greeting and **the right**

behavior for this situation. Not all clients are the same, nor are the situations that will present themselves. In this, leadership becomes important, which I named earlier. Before continuing, I ask you: what do you know about leadership, and what is a leader to you?

Hernan: Leadership is the ability within a person to **organize and direct** others that are below him or her, correct? A leader is a person that takes this role and uses it to **lead a group of people to a goal**.

Patricia: Your answer is great, but there is something that isn't necessarily true – **people don't need to be *below* a leader**. They can **be at the same level**, just that **the leader grabs the reins and helps them find their purpose**. In fact, a true good leader doesn't study people by their **status**, but instead organizes alongside them all and **arrives at a solution**. It's **something that you must aspire to**, Hernan, and **not allow life to pass you by** while you decide what you really desire.

Hernan: Yes, I fully agree. Now, the other subject that we were planning to talk about today was the effective management of staff. What is this about? As I mentioned already, I'm not a manager and I don't have anyone under my charge.

Patricia: The power of management is like leadership – it doesn't matter at what level you are; you can still learn and accomplish great things in your **working environment**. In fact, one study says that **the best leaders and managers** emerged from **the humblest workers** that were once within **the lowest tier** within a company. And do you know why this occurs?

Hernan: Let's see, is it because they've had to see the needs and the problems which **a simple employee** goes through up close, something which isn't the case for those employees who start off higher?

Patricia: Excellent analysis! It's precisely that. They know that the people who arrive assigned to a management position have certain ego problems, and many times **don't have the faintest idea** of how a worker lives or what they survive on. It's for this reason that people who have already gone through these difficulties have a higher chance of filling these positions, since they will know how to work better with the low-ranking employees.

Hernan: The information you're giving me is incredibly valuable, Patricia, truly! And we haven't even started the training yet, have we?

Patricia: Exactly. We're just about to start. That's why you should continue paying attention. I'm going to give you the why, **how to make a change**, what real cases we've witnessed, and also give you a job opportunity that you're going to love.

Hernan: Sounds fascinating! Let's go, then! Let's start **working on transforming me into a better leader**!

CHAPTER 14

NEGOTIATING – ONE-ON-ONE
CREO QUE PUEDES MEJORAR TU OFERTA –
I THINK YOU CAN IMPROVE YOUR OFFER

Vocabulary List

- **¡finalmente llegaste!** = you finally arrived!
- **tengo más de una hora esperando por ti** = I've been waiting for you for over an hour
- **¿por qué tardaste tanto?** = why did you take so long?
- **algo de vida o muerte** = a matter of life and death
- **quiero que hablemos del auto que voy a vender** = I want us to talk about the car I'm selling
- **esa espera me puso de mal humor** = that wait made me cranky
- **estoy muy interesado en comprarlo** = I'm very interested in purchasing it
- **me interesa revisar que todo esté en buen estado** = I want to check that everything is in good shape
- **es un modelo tipo sedán** = it's a sedan type model
- **con un color original azul real** = with a very elegant royal blue original color
- **no lo he usado tanto** = I haven't used it much
- **menos de cien mil kilómetros recorridos** = has less than one hundred thousand kilometers under its belt
- **igual debo confirmar el estado actual del vehículo** = I still have to confirm the current state of the vehicle
- **¿puedes abrir el capó del auto, por favor?** = can you open the hood of the car, please?
- **quiero inspeccionar el motor, las correas y las mangueras** = I want to inspect the engine, the belts and the hoses

107

- **comprobar que están en buen estado** = verify that they're in good shape
- **cauchos también están casi nuevos** = the tires are also almost new
- **el aceite fue cambiado hace poco tiempo** = the oil was changed just a while ago
- **puede subirse al auto y probarlo** = you can hop into the car and try it out
- **yo no tengo problema si conduce un rato** = I don't have any problem with you driving for a while
- **creo que ya terminé de hacer mi inspección** = I think that I'm done with my inspection
- **el auto está prácticamente en perfectas condiciones** = the car is practically in perfect conditions
- **tengo once mil dólares para comprar el auto** = I have eleven thousand dollars to buy the car
- **creí haberle dicho que le costaría quince mil** = I thought I told you before that it would cost fifteen thousand
- **era un muy buen precio para un vehículo así** = it was a very good price for a vehicle like this one.
- **quince mil es demasiado** = fifteen thousand is way too much
- **no está como para pagar quince mil** = it's not in a condition to be paying fifteen thousand
- **habíamos hablado anteriormente y le dije que eran quince mil** = we had spoken previously and I told you it was fifteen thousand
- **además, tengo que hacer el registro de los papeles** = I also have to register the papers
- **no es tan sencillo vender un auto en ese monto en estos tiempos** = it's not easy to sell a car at that price these days
- **¿acaso cree que estoy desesperada?** = do you think I'm desperate?
- **va a tener que buscar otra persona con un auto más económico** = you're going to have to find another person with a cheaper car
- **vamos a acordar un mejor precio** = let's agree on a better price
- **no tiene mucho kilometraje y puede andar por años** = it doesn't

have much mileage and can march for years

- **dudo mucho que vaya a encontrar uno que esté así, tan bien cuidado** = I greatly doubt that you're going to find one that's so well taken care of

- **de resto, se va conmigo a casa** = anything else, it goes back home with me

- **debes aceptar hoy mismo para concretar el negocio** = you must accept today to work out the deal

- **estrecho tu mano para sellar el trato** = I'll shake your hand to seal the deal

Miguel: Así que, ¡finalmente llegaste! **Tengo más de una hora esperando por ti, ¿por qué tardaste tanto?** Ya pensaba irme a casa y olvidarme de esto.

Catherine: Lo siento mucho, señor Miguel, mis padres necesitaban que les hiciera un favor urgente antes de venir. Era **algo de vida o muerte.** Pero lo importante es que ya estoy aquí y que **quiero que hablemos del auto que voy a vender.**

Miguel: Bueno, sí... aunque **esa espera me puso de mal humor.** A ver, señorita Catherine, ¿dónde está estacionado el auto para que empecemos con el negocio? **Estoy muy interesado en comprarlo,** pero **me interesa revisar que todo esté en buen estado** y que no haya ninguna mala sorpresa que me convenza de lo contrario.

Catherine: De acuerdo, sígame. Bueno, aquí está. Como verá, **es un modelo tipo sedán,** del año 2016 y **con un color original azul real,** muy elegante. **No lo he usado tanto,** de hecho, tiene **menos de cien mil kilómetros recorridos,** lo cual es una muy buena noticia para usted.

Miguel: Bueno, sí, es agradable lo que dices, pero **igual debo confirmar el estado actual del vehículo. ¿Puedes abrir el capó del auto, por favor? Quiero inspeccionar el motor, las correas y las mangueras** para comprobar que están en buen estado.

Catherine: Bien, ya puede revisar. Los **cauchos también están casi nuevos** y **el aceite fue cambiado hace poco tiempo.** Cuando termine de ver el motor y las correas **puede subirse al auto y probarlo. Yo no tengo problema si conduce un rato** para ver cómo se siente el auto.

Miguel: Excelente, ¡vamos! De acuerdo, **creo que ya terminé de hacer mi inspección. El auto está prácticamente en perfectas condiciones.** Ahora, me gustaría que habláramos de cuánto va a costarme. **Tengo once mil dólares para comprar el auto.**

Catherine: ¿Once? Eso no es suficiente. **Creí haberle dicho que le costaría quince mil,** y que **era un muy buen precio para un vehículo así.**

Miguel: Quince mil es demasiado, no estoy seguro de que puedas venderlo en ese precio. Es un buen auto y está en buenas condiciones, pero **no está como para pagar quince mil.**

Catherine: Entonces supongo que no va a querer el auto, ¿o qué? **Habíamos hablado anteriormente y le dije que eran quince mil.**

Miguel: Sí, es cierto; pero piensa que, **además, tengo que hacer el registro de los papeles**, y noté que faltan algunas cosas en el papeleo por hacer. Eso será otra inversión, además de que **no es tan sencillo vender un auto en ese monto en estos tiempos.**

Catherine: **¿Acaso cree que estoy desesperada?** Vendiéndolo a once mil, cualquiera podría comprarlo. No es el precio al cual lo voy a vender, lo siento, señor Miguel. **Va a tener que buscar otra persona con un auto más económico.**

Miguel: No, no te vayas. Si es muy poco para ti, entonces **vamos a acordar un mejor precio.** Puedo subir a trece mil, y es lo máximo que puedo dar.

Catherine: Pero, si dijo que tenía solo once... ¿Ahora resulta que tiene trece?

Miguel: Estaba negociando contigo. Seguramente, trece ya se acerca a tu valoración del auto.

Catherine: Sigue estando por debajo. Necesito venderlo a un precio que me beneficie. Le estoy entregando el auto en condiciones casi perfectas, como usted mismo dijo; además, **no tiene mucho kilometraje y puede andar por años.** La verdad es que solamente hay beneficios para usted al adquirir este vehículo. **Dudo mucho que vaya a encontrar uno que esté así, tan bien cuidado.**

Miguel: Mmm... ¿sigue estando bajo entonces? ¿Qué podría convencerte de vendérmelo?

Catherine: Únicamente quince mil dólares. **De resto, se va conmigo a casa.**

Miguel: Última oferta, entonces. Catorce mil doscientos. Es lo más que puedo pagar por un vehículo. Ya, de verdad, es todo lo que tengo, ni un centavo más. Es lo último, y **debes aceptar hoy mismo para concretar el negocio.**

Catherine: ...A ver... Catorce doscientos... Creo que sí. Sí, acepto el trato. Si finiquitamos los detalles, el vehículo es suyo. ¿Cree que podríamos acordar todo hoy mismo?

Miguel: Sí, no hay problema para mí en realizar esos trámites junto a ti. Podemos ir ya, si deseas. Bueno, en este caso, **estrecho tu mano para sellar el trato**. Gracias por aceptar menos de la valoración inicial.

Catherine: No hay problema, necesito el dinero y es una buena oferta. Ahora sí, vayamos a la oficina de registro de vehículos y hagamos lo que se deba hacer. ¡Felicitaciones!, ¡es prácticamente el nuevo dueño del auto!

English

Miguel: So, **you finally arrived! I've been waiting for you for over an hour, why did you take so long?** I was thinking of going home and forgetting this.

Catherine: I'm very sorry, Mr. Miguel, my parents needed me to do them an urgent favor before heading out. It was **a matter of life and death.** But the important part is that I'm here now, and that **I want us to talk about the car I'm selling.**

Miguel: Well, yeah... although **that wait made me cranky.** Let me see, Miss Catherine, where is the car parked so that we can start doing business? **I'm very interested in purchasing it,** but **I want to check that everything is in good shape,** and that there's no bad surprise that will convince me of the contrary.

Catherine: Very well, follow me. Okay, here it is. As you can see, **it's a sedan type model,** of the year 2016 and **with a very elegant royal blue original color. I haven't used it much,** and it actually **has less than one hundred thousand kilometers under its belt,** which is actually great news for you.

Miguel: Well, what you're saying is nice, but **I still have to confirm the current state of the vehicle. Can you open the hood of the car, please? I want to inspect the engine, the belts and the hoses** to **verify that they're in good shape.**

Catherine: Fine, you can check now. **The tires are also almost new,** and **the oil was changed just a while ago.** When you're done looking at the engine and the belts, **you can hop into the car and try it out. I don't have any problem with you driving for a while** so that you can see how the car feels.

Miguel: Excellent, let's go! Actually, **I think that I'm done with my inspection. The car is practically in perfect conditions.** Now, I would like you to let me know how much it's going to cost me. **I have eleven thousand dollars to buy the car.**

Catherine: Eleven? That's not enough. **I thought I told you before that it would cost fifteen thousand,** and that **it was a very good price for a**

113

vehicle like this one.

Miguel: **Fifteen thousand is way too much**, I'm not sure that you'll sell it at that price. It's a good car and is in fine condition, but **it's not in a condition to be paying fifteen thousand**, either.

Catherine: Then I guess you won't want the car, or what? **We had spoken previously and I told you it was fifteen thousand.**

Miguel: Yes, that much is true. But think about the fact that **I also have to register the papers**, and I noted that there's a few things in paperwork still to be done. That would be another investment, as well as the fact that **it's not easy to sell a car at that price these days**.

Catherine: **Do you think I'm desperate?** Selling it at eleven thousand, anyone could buy it. It's not the price at which I'm going to sell it, sorry, Mr. Miguel. **You're going to have to find another person with a cheaper car.**

Miguel: No, don't leave. If it's too little for you, then **let's agree on a better price**. I can raise it to thirteen thousand, and it's the most I can give.

Catherine: But I thought you said you only had eleven? Now you're claiming to have thirteen?

Miguel: I was negotiating with you. Surely at thirteen we're closer now to your valuation of the car.

Catherine: It's still underneath it. I need to sell it at a price that benefits me. I'm handing over the car in almost perfect conditions, as you yourself said; furthermore, **it doesn't have much mileage and can march for years**. The truth is that there are only benefits for you when you purchase this vehicle. **I greatly doubt that you're going to find one that's so well taken care of.**

Miguel: Mmm... is it still low, then? What could convince you to sell it to me?

Catherine: Only fifteen thousand dollars. **Anything else, it goes back home with me.**

Miguel: Last offer, then. Fourteen thousand two hundred. It's the most I can pay for a vehicle. Now it's really all I have, not a single cent more. It's the last of it, and **you must accept today to work out the deal**.

Catherine: ...Let's see... Fourteen two hundred... I think yes. Yeah, I'll accept the deal. If we iron out the details, the vehicle is yours. Do you think we can arrange everything today?

Miguel: Yes, there's no problem for me to do those formalities alongside you. We can go now, if you want. Well in this case, **I'll shake your hand to seal the deal**. Thanks for accepting less.

Catherine: There's no problem, I need the money and it's a good offer. Now, let's go to the vehicle registry office and do what we must. Congratulations, you're practically the new owner of the car!

CHAPTER 15

NEGOTIATING – COMPANY PROJECTS
¿ES FACTIBLE O NO? – IS IT FEASIBLE OR NOT?

Vocabulary List

- **gracias por sacar un momento de su tiempo para mí** = thanks for taking a moment of your time for me
- **tienes un proyecto revolucionario para la empresa** = you have a revolutionary project for the company
- **podría cambiar la manera como hacemos las cosas** = could change the way we do things
- **traer grandes ganancias como nunca antes hemos visto** = bring big earnings like we've never seen before
- **finalmente presentar esto que tengo bajo mi manga desde hace un tiempo** = finally present this that I've been saving up my sleeve for a while now
- **dirigiendo las operaciones en la sección de producción y control de calidad** = directing the operations in the production and quality control section
- **es mejor que vayas directo al punto** = it's best that you get straight to the point
- **finalmente me reúno con usted para discutir una nueva tecnología** = I finally meet with you to discuss a new technology
- **polímeros de ultra altos pesos moleculares** = ultra high-molecular-weight polymers
- **la verdad es que son algo costosos y difíciles de conseguir** = they're somewhat expensive and difficult to obtain
- **me gustaría saber cómo deseas implementarlos en nuestra planta** = I would like to know how you wish to implement them at our plant

- **aquí producimos aditivos para pinturas, recubrimientos industriales y pigmentos** = here we produce paint additives, industrial coatings and pigments
- **la empresa ha tenido problemas con el rendimiento de estos polímeros** = the company has had problems with the yield of these polymers
- **no son sencillos de fabricar** = they're not easy to manufacture
- **nuestros proveedores tampoco están cubriendo la demanda** = our suppliers aren't covering the demand either
- **aumentar este rendimiento en varios factores** = to increase this yield in several factors
- **que supere significativamente estas cifras** = to significantly surpass these numbers
- **¿cómo conseguirías esto? ¿qué deberíamos hacer?** = how would you accomplish this? what must we do?
- **en lugar de seguir comprando los polímeros actuales a varias empresas** = instead of continuing to buy the current polymers to several companies
- **conseguir únicamente el proveedor** = only have to find the supplier
- **pedirle una cantidad determinada** = ask for a specific quantity
- **harían los cálculos necesarios para adaptar la producción** = the necessary calculations would be made to adapt the production
- **le prometo que serían valores más pequeños** = I promise you that the numbers required would be smaller
- **nuestra materia prima actual** = our current raw materials
- **¿la inversión?** = the investment?
- **grandes ideas que surgen de nuestros empleados más brillantes** = great ideas that are born from our most brilliant employees
- **son capaces de traernos enormes ganancias** = are capable of bringing us enormous profits
- **casi nunca son factibles** = almost never are feasible
- **la empresa requiere proyectos factibles** = the company requires feasible projects

- **el espacio para almacenamiento y la carga para los equipos de procesos sería mucho menor** = the storage space and the load for process equipment would be much smaller
- **todo apunta a que sería una inversión con inmensos retornos** = everything is pointing at it being an investment with massive returns
- **¿y los obstáculos?** = and the obstacles?
- **¿nos haga difícil su implementación en nuestros procesos?** = make its implementation difficult in our processes?
- **los conocimientos técnicos** = the technical knowledge
- **los ingenieros de procesos tienen que familiarizarse con el material** = the process engineers would need to familiarize themselves with the material
- **¿cuál es el veredicto?** = what is the verdict?
- **voy a darle un aprobado previo a este proyecto** = I'm going to give this project a pre-approval
- **¡muy pronto estaremos llevando la empresa a nuevos horizontes!** = soon we'll be taking the company towards new horizons!

Spanish

Alejandra: Muy buenas tardes, señor Arturo, es un gusto tenerlo acá presente. **Gracias por sacar un momento de su tiempo para mí.** Era importante que tuviéramos esta conversación.

Arturo: Buenas tardes, señorita Alejandra. Sí, no hay mucho problema por eso de sacar tiempo. He escuchado que **tienes un proyecto revolucionario para la empresa** que **podría cambiar la manera como hacemos las cosas** y **traer grandes ganancias como nunca antes hemos visto.**

Alejandra: Así es, señor Arturo. De hecho, pude haberles dicho a otras personas sobre mi proyecto, pero preferí esperar a que habláramos el día de hoy para **finalmente presentar esto que tengo bajo mi manga desde hace un tiempo.**

Arturo: Ah, es un honor entonces. Bueno, ya sabes que estoy actualmente **dirigiendo las operaciones en la sección de producción y de control de calidad**, así que tienes que ser breve porque debo volver a mi puesto en diez minutos, como máximo. **Es mejor que vayas directo al punto.**

Alejandra: Por supuesto, ¡claro! Bueno, el día de hoy **finalmente me reúno con usted para discutir una nueva tecnología** con la que he tenido contacto durante mi tiempo de estudio con otras empresas aliadas, la cual podría transformar nuestros procesos de fabricación, además de nuestros productos, de forma impresionante. ¿Conoce los **polímeros de ultra altos pesos moleculares?**

Arturo: Bueno sí, en teoría, los conozco; **la verdad es que son algo costosos y difíciles de conseguir...** eso sí, **me gustaría saber cómo deseas implementarlos en nuestra planta.**

Alejandra: De acuerdo. Usted sabe que **aquí producimos aditivos para pinturas, recubrimientos industriales y pigmentos**, y que debemos hacer uso de polímeros a gran escala. Recientemente, **la empresa ha tenido problemas con el rendimiento de estos polímeros**, ya que **no son sencillos de fabricar** y **nuestros proveedores tampoco están cubriendo la demanda.** He descubierto que pueden utilizarse otros polímeros, únicamente los de ultra alto peso molecular, para **aumentar este rendimiento en varios factores** y hacer que la producción no solo vuelva a como era anteriormente, sino **que supere significativamente estas cifras.**

Arturo: Suena muy interesante, Alejandra. **¿Cómo conseguirías esto? ¿Qué deberíamos hacer?**

Alejandra: En lugar de seguir comprando los polímeros actuales a varias empresas, habría que **conseguir únicamente el proveedor** de estos polímeros de ultra alto peso molecular y **pedirle una cantidad determinada.** Luego, se **harían los cálculos necesarios para adaptar la producción** a este nuevo polímero. **Le prometo que serían valores más pequeños** que **nuestra materia prima actual.**

Arturo: Es algo que deberíamos comprobar, pero tiene mucho sentido esto que estás diciendo... Interesante. Ahora, debemos hablar de lo más importante.

Alejandra: ¿Qué? **¿La inversión?**

Arturo: Exactamente. Yo conozco todas estas **grandes ideas que surgen de nuestros empleados más brillantes.** Siempre son muy buenas ideas que cambian todo y que **son capaces de traernos enormes ganancias,** entre otras cosas... pero **casi nunca son factibles. La empresa requiere proyectos factibles,** que nos generen verdaderos ingresos.

Alejandra: Pues en este caso, señor, es totalmente factible. De hecho, puede ver aquí cómo ya he hecho los cálculos. Los costos en materia prima disminuirían en un treinta por ciento, además de que **el espacio para almacenamiento y la carga para los equipos de procesos sería mucho menor;** es posible que nuestra producción diaria aumente también, ya que estos polímeros son de fácil manejo. **Todo apunta a que sería una inversión con inmensos retornos.**

Arturo: ¿Y los obstáculos? ¿Qué nos detiene de utilizar este material? ¿Qué podría presentarse que **nos haga difícil su implementación en nuestros procesos?**

Alejandra: El único inconveniente serían **los conocimientos técnicos.** Hay ciertos cambios que hacer en los procesos, y **los ingenieros de procesos tienen que familiarizarse con el material.** A partir de ese momento, tendremos todo en nuestras manos y no habrá problema. Así que... **¿cuál es el veredicto?** Quiero asegurar una respuesta hoy.

Arturo: Bueno, me gustaría ver más cifras antes de tomar una decisión, pero **voy a darle un aprobado previo a este proyecto**. Me parece excelente. Sigamos adelante y veamos hasta dónde podemos llegar con él.

Alejandra: ¡Gracias, señor Arturo! **¡Muy pronto estaremos llevando la empresa a nuevos horizontes**, se lo prometo!

English

Alejandra: Good afternoon, Mr. Arturo, it's a pleasure to have you here with. **Thanks for taking a moment of your time for me.** It was important for us to have this conversation.

Arturo: Good afternoon, Miss Alejandra. Yes, taking some time out for this isn't much of a problem for me. I've heard that **you have a revolutionary project for the company** that **could change the way we do things** and **bring big earnings like we've never seen before.**

Alejandra: That's right, Mr. Arturo. In fact, I could have told other people about my project, but decided to wait for us to speak today so that I could **finally present this that I've been saving up my sleeve for a while now.**

Arturo: Ah, it's an honor, then. Well, you know that I'm currently **directing the operations in the production and quality control section,** so you must be brief because I have to return to my post in ten minutes tops. **It's best that you get straight to the point.**

Alejandra: Of course, sure! So, today **I finally meet with you to discuss a new technology** which I've been in contact with during my time studying alongside other allied companies, and which could transform our manufacturing processes, as well as our products, in an impressive way. Are you familiar with **ultra high-molecular-weight polymers?**

Arturo: Well yes, in theory I know them, the truth being that **they're somewhat expensive and difficult to obtain...** that said, **I would like to know how you wish to implement them at our plant.**

Alejandra: All right – you know that **here we produce paint additives, industrial coatings and pigments,** and that we must make use of polymers at a great scale. Recently, **the company has had problems with the yield of these polymers,** since **they're not easy to manufacture,** and **our suppliers aren't covering the demand either.** I've discovered that other polymers can be used, exclusively of ultra-high molecular weight, **to increase this yield in several factors,** and to make production not only return to how it was before, but **to significantly surpass these numbers.**

Arturo: It sounds very interesting, Alejandra. **How would you accomplish**

this? What must we do?

Alejandra: Instead of continuing to buy the current polymers to several companies, we would only have to find the supplier of these ultra high-molecular-weight polymers and ask for a specific quantity. Later, the necessary calculations would be made to adapt the production to this new polymer. I promise you that the numbers required would be smaller than our current raw materials.

Arturo: It's something that we would have to verify, but what you're saying makes a lot of sense... Interesting. Now, we must talk about the most important thing.

Alejandra: What? The investment?

Arturo: Exactly. I'm familiar with all of those great ideas that are born from our most brilliant employees. They're always very good ideas that change everything, and which are capable of bringing us enormous profits, among other things... but they almost never are feasible. The company requires feasible projects, which can generate true earnings.

Alejandra: Well in this case, sir, it's totally feasible. In fact, you can see here how I've already done the calculations. The costs of raw material would lower by thirty percent, as well as the storage space and the load for process equipment would be much smaller; it's possible that our daily production would increase too, since these polymers are of easy handling. Everything is pointing at it being an investment with massive returns.

Arturo: And the obstacles? What stops us from using these materials? What could present itself that may make its implementation difficult in our processes?

Alejandra: The only thing would be the technical knowledge. There are certain changes to be made in the processes, and the process engineers would need to familiarize themselves with the material. From that moment onwards, we would have everything in our hands and there would be no problem. Therefore... what is the verdict? I want to ensure an answer for today.

Arturo: Okay, I would like to see more numbers before making a decision, but I'm going to give this project a pre-approval. It seems excellent. Let's continue forward and see where we can go with it.

Alejandra: Thanks, Mr. Arturo! Soon we'll be taking the company

towards new horizons, I promise you!

CHAPTER 16

WORK REVISIONS
VAMOS A CORREGIR ESTE TRABAJO – LET'S CORRECT THIS WORK

Vocabulary List

- **menos mal estás de regreso en tu cubículo** = it's a good thing you're back at your cubicle
- **lidiar con algo respecto a unos papeles que entregué hace un tiempo** = handle something about some papers that I handed in a long time ago
- **¿era algo bueno o algo malo para lo que me estabas buscando?** = were you looking for me over something good or bad?
- **descuida** = relax
- **estuve haciendo una revisión del trabajo** = I simply was doing a revision on the work
- **necesita un par de correcciones antes de ser enviado a nuestros superiores** = it needs a pair of corrections before being sent to our superiors
- **unas cosas urgentes que arreglar** = a few urgent things to fix
- **¿revisiones?** = revisions?
- **¿qué tan urgente es esto?** = how urgent is this?
- **mañana debería estar en manos del director ejecutivo de la empresa** = tomorrow it should be in the hands of the company's chief executive officer
- **¡cuánta presión! esto es demasiado** = that's a lot of pressure! this is too much
- **¿qué debo hacer o cambiar?** = what must I do or change?
- **debería borrar todo y hacerlo de nuevo** = I should delete everything and do it again

- **podrían pasarnos por alto para cualquier promoción o recomendación futura** = we could definitely be ignored for any future promotion or recommendation
- **debemos destacar con este trabajo** = we must shine with this work
- **¿qué es lo que no te gustó tanto del informe que redacté?** = what is it that you didn't like that much about the report I wrote?
- **¿hablé mucho sobre cosas poco relevantes?** = did I talk too much about irrelevant things?
- **¿usé un lenguaje no acorde?** = did I use non-conforming language?
- **¿olvidé citar mis fuentes?** = did I forget to cite my sources?
- **¿no usé referencias confiables?** = didn't I use trustworthy references?
- **tienes unas cuantas sugerencias sobre lo que podemos arreglar** = you have quite a few suggestions about what we could fix
- **fue el lenguaje, más que todo** = it was the language, more than anything else
- **no hablaste de manera formal** = you didn't speak in a formal way
- **encontré errores de gramática y ortografía que podrían dañar la investigación** = I found grammar and spelling mistakes that could damage the research
- **¿tienes tus comentarios sobre el informe a la mano?** = do you have the comments you made on the report on you?
- **olvidé enviarte el documento con los cambios** = I forgot to send you the document with the changes
- **¿qué quisiste decir con lo del formato incorrecto?** = what did you mean with the wrong formatting?
- **un estilo y un formato determinado** = a specific style and formatting
- **van especificados en una guía de redacción** = are specified in a writing guide
- **debe estar en mi correo electrónico** = it must be in my email
- **¡qué error tan tonto!** = what a silly mistake!

- **¡no sé cómo pude cometerlo!** = I'm not sure how I made it
- **no usé lenguaje suficientemente técnico** = I didn't use a sufficiently technical language
- **debes proporcionar los términos utilizados por los expertos** = you must provide the terms used by the experts
- **también he recibido quejas por redactar informes demasiado complicados de leer** = I've also received complaints of writing reports that are too complicated to read
- **hay que buscar el equilibrio, ¿no?** = it's about seeking balance, right?
- **eres la nueva empleada más prometedora que hemos tenido en mucho tiempo** = you're the most promising new employee in a long time
- **agregar más fuentes, junto con tablas y gráficos** = adding more sources, along with charts and graphs
- **podrán citarte en el futuro y presentar tu trabajo en las conferencias** = they could cite you in the future and present your work at conferences
- **en una hora te entregaré la versión final** = in an hour I'll hand you the final version
- **será el mejor informe que hayas visto en tu tiempo trabajando aquí** = it will be the best report you've ever seen in your time working here

Spanish

Spencer: Oh, hola, Penny. **Menos mal estás de regreso en tu cubículo,** tengo horas buscándote por todas partes.

Penny: Hola, Spencer. Sí, tuve que ir a la Dirección de Recursos Humanos para **lidiar con algo respecto a unos papeles que entregué hace un tiempo.** ¿Qué sucede? **¿Era algo bueno o algo malo para lo que me estabas buscando?**

Spencer: Descuida, no era nada malo. Simplemente, **estuve haciendo una revisión del trabajo** que estuviste haciendo esta semana y me parece que **necesita un par de correcciones antes de ser enviado a nuestros superiores.** Nada grave, pero sí **unas cosas urgentes que arreglar.** ¿Tienes tiempo para eso ahora?

Penny: ¿Revisiones? Ya veo. Bueno, sí tengo tiempo, pero **¿qué tan urgente es esto?**

Spencer: Me gustaría decirte que tenemos varios días, pero la verdad es que **mañana debería estar en manos del director ejecutivo de la empresa,** así que ya te podrás imaginar.

Penny: ¡¿Qué?! **¡Cuánta presión! Esto es demasiado.** Y, **¿qué debo hacer o cambiar?** No pensé que era para el director ejecutivo. **Debería borrar todo y hacerlo de nuevo,** para que le guste. Y, ¿si no le gusta? ¿Me echarán de la empresa? ¡Qué terrible!

Spencer: No, nada de eso, pero sí **podrían pasarnos por alto para cualquier promoción o recomendación futura. Debemos destacar con este trabajo,** ¿no crees?

Penny: Sí, estoy lista. Cuéntame, **¿qué es lo que no te gustó tanto del informe que redacté? ¿Hablé mucho sobre cosas poco relevantes? ¿Usé un lenguaje no acorde? ¿Olvidé citar mis fuentes? ¿No usé referencias confiables?**

Spencer: Hmm, parece que **tienes unas cuantas sugerencias sobre lo que podemos arreglar.** Creo que **fue el lenguaje, más que todo. No hablaste de manera formal.** Además, **encontré errores de gramática y ortografía que podrían dañar la investigación.** El contenido es muy bueno, pero debemos corregir cómo lo expresaste, ¿me entiendes?

Penny: Sí, te entiendo a la perfección. **¿Tienes tus comentarios sobre el informe a la mano?** ¿O me vas a ir diciendo poco a poco? De ambas maneras me sirve.

Spencer: Ah, ¡cierto! **Olvidé enviarte el documento con los cambios.** Ya te lo voy a enviar desde mi teléfono celular. De acuerdo, listo. Bueno, vamos a trabajar de ambas maneras —vas a leer los comentarios, pero también voy a seguir muy de cerca tu trabajo—.

Penny: Perfecto, ya estoy leyendo los primeros comentarios. A ver, **¿qué quisiste decir con lo del formato incorrecto?**

Spencer: Ah, bueno. La empresa nos exige que creemos los informes con **un estilo y un formato determinado,** los cuales **van especificados en una guía de redacción.** ¿Tienes esa guía?

Penny: Sí, **debe estar en mi correo electrónico. ¡Qué error tan tonto! No sé cómo pude cometerlo.** Ya lo encontré, voy a aplicar el formato al texto para que esté listo para su entrega. Ahora, en el siguiente comentario, dices que **no usé lenguaje suficientemente técnico.**

Spencer: Sí, no fuiste muy técnica. **Debes proporcionar los términos utilizados por los expertos** y el personal dentro de la empresa, especialmente cuando hablas de los equipos y programas involucrados.

Penny: Mmm, sí, tienes toda la razón. Fue una gran falla. A veces es difícil asegurar que estoy usando el lenguaje correcto, porque **también he recibido quejas por redactar informes demasiado complicados de leer.**

Spencer: Supongo que **hay que buscar el equilibrio, ¿no?** Nunca es fácil cuando estás comenzando, pero me dicen que **eres la nueva empleada más prometedora que hemos tenido en mucho tiempo.** Siéntete orgullosa de eso.

Penny: ¡Gracias, es cierto! Ahora, el último comentario importante que escribiste aquí fue el de **agregar más fuentes, junto con tablas y gráficos.**

Spencer: Correcto, debes añadir más de esos. De esa forma, los lectores —incluyendo el director ejecutivo— van a tomar más en serio todo lo que estás diciendo. Incluso, **podrán citarte en el futuro y presentar tu trabajo en las conferencias.** Y, cuando digo conferencias, no solo hablo de las de la empresa, sino también aquellas nacionales o internacionales que se llevan a cabo.

Penny: ¿En serio podrían mostrarlo ante el país y el mundo? ¡Qué impresionante! Eso sería excelente. Bueno, **en una hora te entregaré la versión final,** ¿de acuerdo? **Será el mejor informe que hayas visto en tu tiempo trabajando aquí.**

Spencer: Gracias, Penny. ¡Así será! Suerte con eso, ¡nos vemos en una hora!

English

Spencer: Oh, hello, Penny. **It's a good thing you're back at your cubicle,** I've been looking for you everywhere for hours.

Penny: Hi, Spencer. Yes, I had to go to the human resources management to **handle something about some papers that I handed in a long time ago.** What is going on? **Were you looking for me over something good or bad?**

Spencer: **Relax,** it wasn't anything bad. **I simply was doing a revision on the work** you were performing this week, and it seems that **it needs a pair of corrections before being sent to our superiors.** Nothing serious, but definitely **a few urgent things to fix.** Do you have time for that now?

Penny: **Revisions?** I see. Well, I have time but, **how urgent is this?**

Spencer: I would love to tell you that we have several days, but the truth is that **tomorrow it should be in the hands of the company's chief executive officer,** so you can imagine.

Penny: What?! **That's a lot of pressure! This is too much.** And **what must I do or change?** I never thought it would be for the chief executive. I **should delete everything and do it again,** so that he likes it. And if he doesn't? Will I be fired from the company? What a horrible thought!

Spencer: No, none of that, but **we could definitely be ignored for any future promotion or recommendation. We must shine with this work,** don't you think?

Penny: Yes, I'm ready. Tell me, **what is it that you didn't like that much about the report I wrote? Did I talk too much about irrelevant things? Did I use non-conforming language? Did I forget to cite my sources? Didn't I use trustworthy references?**

Spencer: Hmm, it looks like **you have quite a few suggestions about what we could fix.** I think **it was the language, more than anything else. You didn't speak in a formal way.** Furthermore, **I found grammar and spelling mistakes that could damage the research.** The content is very good, but we must correct how you expressed it, do you understand?

Penny: Yes, I understand perfectly. **Do you have the comments you made on the report on you?** Or will you tell me one by one? Both ways work for me.

Spencer: Ah, sure! **I forgot to send you the document with the changes.** I'm going to send it now from my cell phone. All right, done. Now, let's work in both ways – you're going to read the comments, but I'm also going to follow your work closely.

Penny: Perfect, I'm reading the first comments now. Let's see, **what did you mean with the wrong formatting?**

Spencer: Oh, well. The company demands that we create our reports with **a specific style and formatting,** which **are specified in a writing guide.** Do you have that guide?

Penny: Yes, **it must be in my email. What a silly mistake! I'm not sure how I made it.** I've found it, so now I'm going to apply the formatting to the text so that it can be ready for submission. Now, the next comment, you say **I didn't use a sufficiently technical language.**

Spencer: Yes, you weren't technical enough. **You must provide the terms used by the experts** and staff within the company. Especially when you're talking about the equipment and programs involved.

Penny: Mmm, yeah, you're absolutely right. It was a big flaw. Sometimes it's difficult to make sure I'm using the right language, because **I've also received complaints of writing reports that are too complicated to read.**

Spencer: I guess **it's about seeking balance, right?** It's never easy when you're starting off, but I've been told that **you're the most promising new employee in a long time.** Feel proud of that.

Penny: Thanks, it's true! Now, the last important comment that you wrote here was about **adding more sources, along with charts and graphs.**

Spencer: Correct, you should add more of those. That way, readers – including the executive officer – will take everything you're saying more seriously. Furthermore, **they could cite you in the future and present your work at conferences.** And when I say conferences, I don't just mean those at the company, but also the national and international ones that take place.

Penny: Could they really show it before the country and the world? How amazing! That would be excellent. Well, **in an hour I'll hand you the final version,** all right? **It will be the best report you've ever seen in your time**

working here.

Spencer: Thanks, Penny. You bet! Good luck with that, see you in an hour!

CHAPTER 17

INTERNSHIP EVALUATION

ESTO DECIDIRÁ TU FUTURO EN LA INDUSTRIA – THIS WILL DECIDE YOUR FUTURE IN THE INDUSTRY

Vocabulary List

- **no te había vuelto a ver desde tu primer día** = I hadn't seen you again since your first day
- **voy a suponer que estás buscando la evaluación** = I'm guessing you've come looking for the evaluation
- **las obligaciones de la pasantía** = the internship obligations
- **me he sentido muy agradecido con usted** = I have felt very thankful to you
- **voy a recordar mi experiencia aquí para siempre** = I'm going to remember my experience here forever
- **vengo a realizar la evaluación final de la pasantía** = I'm here to take part in the final internship evaluation
- **agradezco que tengas esa percepción de la empresa** = I'm thankful for you to have that perception of the company
- **¿estás listo para contestar las preguntas?** = are you ready to answer the questions?
- **será sencillo todo, pero debes ser sincero** = everything will be simple, but you have to be honest
- **es lo último que me falta para culminar esta pasantía** = it's the last thing remaining to finish this internship
- **¿puedes describir tu experiencia en la empresa con una única palabra?** = can you describe your experience at the company with a single word?
- **comenzaran a hacerme sentir como parte de una gran familia** = started making me feel as if I was part of a great family

- **nunca me faltó colaboración para poder aprender a usar los sistemas** = I never lacked cooperation to learn how to use the systems
- **siempre hubo alguien acompañándome** = there was always someone accompanying me
- **asegurándose de que me iba bien** = making sure I was doing well
- **¿hubo algo que no te haya gustado o que cambiarías?** = was there something that you didn't like or which you'd change?
- **no cambiaría nada** = I wouldn't change anything
- **disfruté las instalaciones** = enjoyed the facilities
- **¿cómo piensas usar esta experiencia para crecer en tu carrera?** = how do you plan to use this experience to grow in your career?
- **¿le dio esta pasantía un giro a tu vida profesional o simplemente fue un paso más?** = did this internship give a new turn to your professional life, or was it simply an additional step?
- **creo que esta experiencia me ayudará a entender cómo es la vida realmente en las empresas** = I think that this experience will help me understand what life is really like in the companies
- **pude ver realmente qué es lo que hacemos** = I was able to see what we really do
- **qué voy a hacer en un futuro** = what I'm going to do in the future
- **entender mejor mi rol en la industria** = better understanding my role in the industry
- **observar las dificultades de todas las cosas que vienen por delante** = observing the difficulties I have coming up ahead
- **entender mejor lo que debo aprender antes de graduarme y convertirme en un empleado más** = better understand what I must learn before graduating and becoming another employee
- **me ayudó a prepararme para trabajar en equipo con otros profesionales** = helped me learn to prepare myself for working as a team with other professionals
- **¿cuál fue tu momento profesional más memorable dentro de la empresa?** = what was your most memorable professional moment within the company?
- **recibí una gran bienvenida. Hubo muy buena recepción** =

received a great welcome. There was such a good reception

- **una gran fiesta de cumpleaños anticipada** = it was like a great birthday party in advance
- **me sentí como parte de algo especial** = I felt like part of something special
- **algo que intento cultivar en la oficina** = It's something that I try to cultivate at the office
- **¿cuál sería tu evaluación de ti mismo en estos ocho meses de pasantía?** = what would be your evaluation of yourself in these eight months of internship?
- **un valor del uno al diez** = a value between one to ten
- **no logré cumplir todos los objetivos que me propuse** = I didn't manage to accomplish all of the objectives I set myself
- **tu actitud profesional ha sido genial** = your professional attitude has been excellent
- **has logrado enormes resultados** = you've accomplished enormous results
- **me aseguraré de darte una recomendación** = I'll make sure to give you a recommendation
- **¡sal allá afuera a comerte el mundo!** = go out there and show the world what you're made of!

136

Elena: ¿Cómo te va, Jack? Es un placer verte por acá, **no te había vuelto a ver desde tu primer día...** ¿hace cuánto fue eso? ¿Qué te trae por aquí el día de hoy? **Voy a suponer que estás buscando la evaluación.**

Jack: Hola, señora Elena, estoy muy bien, ¿y usted? Sí, no he tenido tiempo de pasar por acá por **las obligaciones de la pasantía,** el informe y todas esas cosas. Igualmente, **me he sentido muy agradecido con usted** por haberme traído a esta empresa y **voy a recordar mi experiencia aquí para siempre.** Y, bueno, sí... **vengo a realizar la evaluación final de la pasantía,** ¿tendrá tiempo ahora mismo o prefiere que regrese en unas horas?

Elena: Muy bonitas palabras, Jack. **Agradezco que tengas esa percepción de la empresa.** De acuerdo, creo que sí tengo media hora para dedicarla a esta evaluación. Ahora, **¿estás listo para contestar las preguntas? Será sencillo todo, pero debes ser sincero.**

Jack: Sí, estoy listo. **Es lo último que me falta para culminar esta pasantía,** así que he estado preparándome.

Elena: Perfecto. Voy a comenzar. Vamos con la primera pregunta: **¿puedes describir tu experiencia en la empresa con una única palabra?** De ser así, ¿cuál y por qué?

Jack: De acuerdo, sí puedo usar una palabra. Me gustaría utilizar la palabra *familiar* para esta respuesta. Digo «familiar» porque, al llegar, no pasaron ni diez minutos para que las personas de mi departamento de la empresa **comenzaran a hacerme sentir como parte de una gran familia. Nunca me faltó colaboración para poder aprender a usar los sistemas,** para saber los horarios y para hacer amigos. Fue muy genial, **siempre hubo alguien acompañándome y asegurándose de que me iba bien.**

Elena: Excelente, me encanta saber eso. Ahora, la segunda pregunta: **¿hubo algo que no te haya gustado o que cambiarías?** De ser así, ¿qué?

Jack: En realidad, mi tiempo acá fue perfecto, **no cambiaría nada.** Desde el primer momento hasta el último lo disfruté, y también **disfruté las instalaciones.**

Elena: ¿Seguro? De acuerdo. Tercera pregunta para ti: **¿cómo piensas**

usar esta experiencia para crecer en tu carrera? ¿Le dio esta pasantía un giro a tu vida profesional o simplemente fue un paso más?

Jack: Interesantes preguntas. Bueno, para comenzar, **creo que esta experiencia me ayudará a entender cómo es la vida realmente en las empresas** de nuestra industria. **Pude ver realmente qué es lo que hacemos** y **qué voy a hacer en un futuro.** Disfruté poder **entender mejor mi rol en la industria**, además de **observar las dificultades de todas las cosas que vienen por delante.** Ahora, sí pienso que esta pasantía le dio un giro a mi carrera. Voy a **entender mejor lo que debo aprender antes de graduarme y convertirme en un empleado más,** y esto **me ayudó a prepararme para trabajar en equipo con otros profesionales.**

Elena: De acuerdo, quedan solo dos preguntas más. Cuarta pregunta: **¿cuál fue tu momento profesional más memorable dentro de la empresa?**

Jack: Creo que sería el instante en el que entré y **recibí una gran bienvenida. Hubo muy buena recepción** y, de hecho, los otros tres pasantes que entraron lo disfrutaron igual que yo. Todos estaban muy felices de tenernos acá, y era como **una gran fiesta de cumpleaños anticipada. Me sentí como parte de algo especial.**

Elena: ¡Que bueno saberlo, Jack! Es **algo que intento cultivar en la oficina**, un gran trato hacia todos los compañeros, ¡sin importar qué rango o edad tengan! Última pregunta, y esta es la más importante de todas: **¿cuál sería tu evaluación de ti mismo en estos ocho meses de pasantía?** ¿Puedes ponerle **un valor del uno al diez**?

Jack: ¡Vaya! Esa pregunta sí que es interesante. Bueno, a ver, pienso que merezco un siete de diez.

Elena: ¿Siete? Justifica ese resultado, por favor.

Jack: Pienso que hubo veces que llegué tarde a trabajar y, aunque no fueron muchas, sí sucedió. También tardé un poco en entregar mi informe final y no fue hasta el último día, hoy, cuando lo tuve listo. Además, **no logré cumplir todos los objetivos que me propuse.**

Elena: Bueno, Jack. Gracias por responder a todo. Quiero que sepas que, a pesar de tu autoevaluación, yo pienso que mereces un diez. Has sido, para mí, el mejor pasante que ha pasado por aquí. **Tu actitud profesional ha sido genial, has logrado enormes resultados**, y me aseguraré de darte

una recomendación para que vengas a formar parte de nuestro equipo apenas te gradúes.

Jack: ¿Es en serio?

Elena: Sí. Así que, ¡**sal allá afuera a comerte el mundo**! Suerte... y nunca cambies tu actitud.

Jack: ¡Gracias, señora Elena! ¡Es un enorme honor! ¡Lo haré!

English

Elena: How's it going, Jack. It's a pleasure to see you come by, since **I hadn't seen you again since your first day**... how long ago was that? What brings you here today? **I'm guessing you've come looking for the evaluation.**

Jack: Hello, Mrs. Elena, I'm doing very well, and you? Yes, I haven't had much time to come by here because of **the internship obligations**, the report and all of those things. Still, **I have felt very thankful to you** for bringing me to this company, and **I'm going to remember my experience here forever.** And well, yes... **I'm here to take part in the final internship evaluation**, do you have time right now or do you prefer that I come back in a few hours?

Elena: Very beautiful words, Jack. **I'm thankful for you to have that perception of the company.** Okay then, I think I do have half an hour to dedicate to this evaluation. Now, **are you ready to answer the questions? Everything will be simple, but you have to be honest.**

Jack: Yes, I'm ready. **It's the last thing remaining to finish this internship**, so I've been preparing myself.

Elena: Perfect. I'll begin. Let's start with the first question: **can you describe your experience at the company with a single word?** If so, which one and why?

Jack: Very well, I can use one word. I would like to use the word *family* for this answer. I say 'family' because when I arrived, not even ten minutes had passed before people of my company department **started making me feel as if I was part of a great family. I never lacked cooperation to learn how to use the systems**, to learn the schedules and to make new friends. It was amazing, **there was always someone accompanying me** and making sure I was doing well.

Elena: Excellent, I love to hear that. Now, second question: **was there something that you didn't like or which you'd change?** If so, what?

Jack: Truthfully, my time here was perfect, and **I wouldn't change anything**. From the first moment until the last I enjoyed it, and also enjoyed the facilities.

Elena: Are you sure? All right. Third question for you: **how do you plan to use this experience to grow in your career? Did this internship give a new turn to your professional life, or was it simply an additional step?**

Jack: Interesting questions. Well, to begin, **I think that this experience will help me understand what life is really like in the companies** of our industry. **I was able to see what we really do** and **what I'm going to do in the future.** I enjoyed **better understanding my role in the industry,** as well as **observing the difficulties I have coming up ahead.** Now, I think that this internship gave a marked a turning point for my career. **I'll better understand what I must learn before graduating and becoming another employee,** and this **helped me learn to prepare myself for working as a team with other professionals.**

Elena: Fine, now there's only two more questions. Fourth question: **what was your most memorable professional moment within the company?**

Jack: I think that it would be the moment in which I entered and **received a great welcome. There was such a good reception**, and in fact the other three interns that joined enjoyed it as much as I did. Everyone was so happy to have us here, and **it was like a great birthday party in advance. I felt like part of something special.**

Elena: ¡That's amazing to know, Jack! **It's something that I try to cultivate at the office**, a great treatment towards co-workers, no matter what rank or age they are! Last question, and this is the most important of them all – **what would be your evaluation of yourself in these eight months of internship?** Can you place **a value between one to ten**?

Jack: Yikes! That question sure is interesting. Okay, let's see, I think I deserve a seven out of ten.

Elena: Seven? Justify that result, please.

Jack: I think that there were times when I arrived late to work, and although it wasn't many times, it did happen. I also took some time to submit my final report, and it wasn't until the last day, today, when I had it ready. Furthermore, **I didn't manage to accomplish all of the objectives I set myself.**

Elena: Well, Jack. Thanks for answering everything. I want you to know that, despite your self-assessment, I believe you deserve a ten. You have been, to me, the best intern that has come here. **Your professional attitude has been excellent, you've accomplished enormous results,** and **I'll make sure to give you a recommendation** so that you can come and form part of our team once you've gradated.

Jack: Are you serious?

Elena: Yes. Now **go out there and show the world what you're made of!** Good luck... and never change your approach.

Jack: Thanks, Mrs. Elena! It's a massive honor! I'll do it!

CHAPTER 18

EXPLAINING A MISTAKE

¡LO LAMENTO MUCHO, FUE UN GRAVE ERROR! – I'M SO SORRY, IT WAS A TERRIBLE MISTAKE!

Vocabulary List

- **eso que pasó esta mañana es inaceptable dentro de la empresa** = the event that took place this morning is unacceptable within the company
- **pudiera considerarse un acto criminal** = could be considered a criminal act
- **podría llamar a la policía y presentar cargos, y estarías preso en poco tiempo** = I could call the police and press charges, and you would be arrested in a short time
- **voy a tener que llamar a las autoridades inmediatamente** = I will have to call the authorities immediately
- **todo es un malentendido, ¡puedo explicarlo!** = it's all a misunderstanding, I can explain!
- **no me parece un malentendido** = it doesn't seem like a misunderstanding
- **conductor de montacargas** = forklift driver
- **bajo la influencia del alcohol** = under the influence of alcohol
- **debido a tu estado de embriaguez** = because of your state of drunkenness
- **derribaste numerosas estanterías llenas de mercancía de alto costo** = you knocked down several pallet racks full of expensive goods
- **destrozos valorados en varias decenas de miles de dólares** = destruction valued in several tens of thousands of dollars
- **acabaste con, al menos, una cuarta parte de los electrodomésticos** = you wrecked at least a quarter of the

electrical appliances

- **destrozaste muchos equipos que estaban listos para ser entregados** = destroyed many pieces of equipment that were ready to be delivered
- **lidiar con este problema** = deal with this problem
- **es cierto que causé un gran daño a la empresa** = it's true that I caused massive damages to the company
- **esto es imperdonable** = this is unforgivable
- **¡estás fracasando!** = you're failing!
- **¿la mercancía estaba asegurada?** = were the goods insured?
- **no hemos confirmado si el seguro va a cubrir esto** = we haven't confirmed if the insurance will cover this
- **nunca he fallado antes** = I've never made a mistake before
- **lo que hiciste fue demasiado** = what you did was too much
- **hice algo terrible, muy estúpido** = I did something terrible, very stupid
- **estoy pasando por un muy mal momento** = I'm going through a very bad moment
- **me está yendo muy mal** = everything's going so badly for me
- **cada vez tengo más deudas y problemas** = every time I seem to have more debts and problems
- **últimamente estoy más deprimido y sin saber cómo salir de esta situación difícil** = lately I'm more depressed and without having an idea of how to get out of this difficult situation
- **es difícil seguir viniendo a pesar de lo que pasa en casa** = it's difficult to continue coming here despite what is going on at home
- **puede llamar al terapeuta de la empresa y consultarle** = you can call the company's therapist and check it out with him
- **parece que estás sufriendo de una seria depresión** = it seems that you're suffering from a serious depression
- **alcoholismo agudo** = acute alcoholism
- **debo pagar las consecuencias de alguna forma** = I must pay the consequences somehow

- **terminaría de arruinar mi vida** = it would finish ruining my life
- **necesito que recompenses a la empresa por este terrible acontecimiento** = I need you to compensate the company for this terrible event
- **buscaría maneras de reparar los equipos que se hayan dañado con la caída** = seek ways to repair the equipment that has been damaged with the fall
- **espero que se pueda recuperar lo que destruí** = I hope I can help recover what I destroyed
- **jamás volverá a suceder** = it will never happen again
- **gracias por asumir tu responsabilidad** = thank you for accepting your responsibility

Spanish

Bárbara: Edward, voy a necesitar que seas completamente sincero: **eso que pasó esta mañana es inaceptable dentro de la empresa** y **pudiera considerarse un acto criminal.** Podría llamar a la policía y presentar cargos, y **estarías preso en poco tiempo.** Exijo una explicación, o **voy a tener que llamar a las autoridades inmediatamente.**

Edward: ¡Espere, por favor! **Todo es un malentendido, ¡puedo explicarlo!**

Bárbara: No me parece un malentendido, la verdad. Viniste a tu trabajo de **conductor de montacargas bajo la influencia del alcohol** y, **debido a tu estado de embriaguez, derribaste numerosas estanterías llenas de mercancía de alto costo,** causando **destrozos valorados en varias decenas de miles de dólares. Acabaste con, al menos, una cuarta parte de los electrodomésticos** que teníamos en el almacén, **destrozaste muchos equipos que estaban listos para ser entregados** a nuestros clientes y ahora debemos **lidiar con este problema,** con la época navideña acercándose rápidamente.

Edward: Sí, **es cierto que causé un gran daño a la empresa** y que la noche anterior había consumido una gran cantidad de alcohol, pero era mi cumpleaños y me hicieron una fiesta sorpresa, y...

Bárbara: ¡No me interesa! **Esto es imperdonable.** ¿Crees que porque ayer era tu cumpleaños te vas a salvar de las consecuencias? Si esta es tu manera de detenerme de llamar a la policía, **¡estás fracasando!**

Edward: ¡Por favor, espere a que podamos mirarlo desde otro punto de vista! **¿La mercancía estaba asegurada?**

Bárbara: Sí, pero **no hemos confirmado si el seguro va a cubrir esto.** Esa incertidumbre es la única razón por la que aún tienes trabajo.

Edward: Señora Bárbara, recuerde que tengo siete años trabajando fielmente con ustedes, incluso en días libres, vacaciones y domingos. **Nunca he fallado antes,** ¡entiéndalo, por favor!

Bárbara: Es cierto, pero **lo que hiciste fue demasiado.** ¿En qué estabas pensando cuando viniste a trabajar en esas condiciones? Fue una estupidez, ¡y mira lo que causó!

146

Edward: Sí, **hice algo terrible, muy estúpido.** No puedo justificarlo, yo... **estoy pasando por un muy mal momento.** Mi cumpleaños, anoche, fue la primera vez que alguien se ha acordado de mí en mucho tiempo —**me está yendo muy mal**—. Mi esposa me dejó hace dos meses, llevándose a mis hijos, y **cada vez tengo más deudas y problemas.** Sí, tomé de más, pero fue debido a que **últimamente estoy más deprimido y sin saber cómo salir de esta situación difícil.** No he querido faltar al trabajo, pero **es difícil seguir viniendo a pesar de lo que pasa en casa.**

Bárbara: Mmm... no sabía que esto estaba sucediendo en casa. Pero tampoco tengo cómo corroborarlo. ¿Puedes demostrar que todo está ocurriendo de alguna manera?

Edward: Sí, **puede llamar al terapeuta de la empresa y consultarle.** He estado yendo a consulta con él.

Bárbara: Lo haré, dame unos minutos... De acuerdo, Edward. **Parece que estás sufriendo de una seria depresión**, la cual ha provocado un **alcoholismo agudo.** Esto no suena nada bien. Por un momento, incluso puedo sentir que lo que pasó en el almacén no es tan grave.

Edward: No, señora Bárbara, **debo pagar las consecuencias de alguna forma.** Solo no llame a la policía, por favor. Eso sería lo peor que podría ocurrirme en estos momentos. **Terminaría de arruinar mi vida.** No quiero que mis hijos sepan que estuve en la cárcel; terminaría de perderlos.

Bárbara: No voy a llamar a la policía, ¿de acuerdo? Pero **necesito que recompenses a la empresa por este terrible acontecimiento.** ¿Qué sugieres?

Edward: Sí... puedo pagarlo con trabajo, trabajando horas extra. También ayudaría a arreglar el desastre que causé y **buscaría maneras de reparar los equipos que se hayan dañado con la caída.** Es lo mínimo que puedo hacer.

Bárbara: De acuerdo. Además, deberás recibir un pequeño descuento a tu salario por seis meses. No será mucho, pero será suficiente para que ya no tengas que preocuparte por un problema legal. Yo soy tu supervisora directa, pero si no aceptas y se enteran los gerentes o directores, se acabó todo para ti.

Edward: Está bien. Acepto. Voy a necesitar que hagamos un contrato, pero está bien, no tengo otra opción. Gracias, señora Bárbara. No es fácil, y no quería que me afectara así, pero **espero que se pueda recuperar lo que destruí. Jamás volverá a suceder.**

Bárbara: No hay problema, Edward. Saldremos de esto, ya verás. Ahora, ve a ayudar a arreglar lo que rompiste y luego tómate el día. Pronto te haré un nuevo contrato. **Gracias por asumir tu responsabilidad.**

English

Barbara: Edward, I'm going to need you to be completely honest – **the event that took place this morning is unacceptable within the company and could be considered a criminal act. I could call the police and press charges, and you would be arrested in a short time.** I demand an explanation, or **I will have to call the authorities immediately.**

Edward: Wait, please! **It's all a misunderstanding, I can explain!**

Barbara: **It doesn't seem like a misunderstanding**, to be honest. You came to your job as a **forklift driver under the influence of alcohol**, and **because of your state of drunkenness you knocked down several pallet racks full of expensive goods**, causing **destruction valued in several tens of thousands of dollars. You wrecked at least a quarter of the electrical appliances** we had in the warehouse, **destroyed many pieces of equipment that were ready to be delivered** to our clients, and we have to **deal with this problem** now, with the Christmas period approaching quickly.

Edward: Yes, **it's true that I caused massive damages to the company**, and that last night I consumed a huge amount of alcohol, but it was my birthday and they threw a surprise party for me and...

Barbara: I don't care! **This is unforgivable.** Do you think that because it was your birthday yesterday you're going to be saved from the consequences? If this is your way of stopping me from calling the police, **you're failing!**

Edward: Please, wait until we can look at it from another point of view! **Were the goods insured?**

Barbara: Yes, but **we haven't confirmed if the insurance will cover this**. That uncertainty is the only reason why you still have a job.

Edward: Mrs. Barbara, remember that I've been working here for you faithfully for seven years, even on days off, vacations and Sundays. **I've never made a mistake before**, understand it, please!

Barbara: It's true, but **what you did was too much.** What were you thinking when you came to work in those conditions? It was an act of stupidity, and look at what it caused.

Edward: Yes, **I did something terrible, very stupid**. I can't justify it, I... **I'm going through a very bad moment**. My birthday last night was the first time somebody has remembered me for the longest time – **everything's going so badly for me**. My wife left me two months ago, taking my children with her, and **every time I seem to have more debts and problems**. Yes, I drank too much, but it was due to the fact that **lately I'm more depressed and without having an idea of how to get out of this difficult situation**. I haven't wanted to miss work, but **it's difficult to continue coming here despite what is going on at home**.

Barbara: Mmm... I had no idea that this was happening at home. But I don't have a way to verify what you're saying. Can you demonstrate that this is all taking place somehow?

Edward: Yes, **you can call the company's therapist and check it out with him**. I've been going to appointments with him.

Barbara: I will, give me a few minutes... All right, Edward. **It seems that you're suffering from a serious depression**, which has caused a bout of **acute alcoholism**. This doesn't sound good at all. For a moment, I can even feel that what happened at the warehouse isn't so serious.

Edward: No, Mrs. Barbara. **I must pay the consequences somehow**. Just don't call the police, please. That would be the worst thing that could happen to me at this moment. **It would finish ruining my life**. I don't want my kids to know that I was in prison; I would lose them for good.

Barbara: I'm not calling the police, okay? But **I need you to compensate the company for this terrible event**. What do you suggest?

Edward: Yeah... I can pay it with work, working extra hours. I would also help fix the disaster I created and **seek ways to repair the equipment that has been damaged with the fall**. It's the least I could do.

Barbara: Very well. Also, you will receive a small discount of your salary for six months. It won't be a lot, but just enough for you not to have to worry about a legal problem. I'm your direct supervisor, but if you don't accept and the managers or directors find out, it's all over for you.

Edward: It's fine, I accept. I'm going to need us to make a contract, but it's okay, I have no choice. Thank you, Mrs. Barbara. It isn't easy, and I didn't want it to affect me like it did, but **I hope I can help recover what I**

destroyed. It will never happen again.

Barbara: No problem, Edward. We'll get out of this, you'll see. Now go help fix what you broke, and then take the day off. I'll soon write a new contract for you. **Thank you for accepting your responsibility.**

CHAPTER 19

FIRING SOMEBODY

QUE TENGAS BUENA SUERTE EN OTRA EMPRESA – GOOD LUCK AT ANOTHER COMPANY

Vocabulary List

- **disculpe por llegar un poquito tarde a su cita** = I'm sorry for arriving a bit late to the appointment
- **necesitaba comunicarte algo** = I needed to inform you of something
- **¿es algo serio?** = is it something serious?
- **siento el ambiente algo tenso** = I feel the tension in the atmosphere
- **reestructuración** = restructuring
- **los departamentos han sido reorganizados** = the departments have been reorganized
- **algunos cargos se han cambiado o eliminado por completo** = some positions have been changed or eliminated entirely
- **ilustraban de manera detallada y específica** = illustrated, specifically and in detail
- **las personas de las que vamos a prescindir** = the people we are going to lay off
- **lamentándolo mucho** = with great regret
- **debo informarte que no vamos a requerir tus servicios a partir del final de este mes** = I must inform you that we are no longer going to require your services starting from the end of this month
- **tu cargo ha sido fusionado con el de supervisor** = your position has been merged with that of the customer service supervisor
- **un especialista de la capital** = a specialist from the capital

- **arreglar tus asuntos** = arrange your affairs
- **agradecimiento** = appreciation
- **un bono en tu indemnización** = a bonus in your severance pay
- **creo que nunca he fallado en mis responsabilidades** = I believe I've never failed in my responsibilities
- **me gustaría que reconsideraran esta decisión** = I would like for this decision to be reconsidered
- **mil disculpas** = I beg forgiveness
- **estás entre mis mejores empleados** = you are among my best employees
- **no soy el que decide ni el que da la orden** = I'm not the one who decides or gives the order
- **brindarte una recomendación para tus futuros empleos** = provide you a recommendation for your future jobs
- **actualmente debo cubrir los gastos de mi hogar** = I currently have to cover the expenses at home
- **crisis de desempleo** = unemployment crisis
- **probablemente me mantenga desempleada** = I will probably stay unemployed
- **beneficios del estado para desempleados** = state benefits for the unemployed
- **no podré calificar para esos beneficios** = I won't qualify for those benefits
- **poseo una vivienda y automóvil propio** = I own a home and car
- **baja prioridad** = low priority
- **entre en efecto** = comes into effect
- **decirles a mis hijos que fui despedida** = tell my kids I've been fired
- **¡ha salvado a mi familia!** = you've saved my family!
- **sé que podrás recuperar tu camino** = I know you'll be able to get back on your path
- **todas las historias deben llegar a su fin** = all stories must reach their ending
- **nunca lo olvidaré** = I'll never forget you

Spanish

June: Buen día, señor Harry, ¿cómo está? **Disculpe por llegar un poquito tarde a su cita,** estaba terminando unas tareas de la oficina. Me avisaron esta mañana que necesitaba verme.

Harry: Sí, June. Gracias por venir. No te preocupes, toma asiento. Así es, **necesitaba comunicarte algo.**

June: A ver, ¿qué será? **¿Es algo serio? Siento el ambiente algo tenso,** la verdad.

Harry: Bueno, June, es importante que hablemos un poco de la empresa y una **reestructuración** que se está llevando a cabo en este momento. La directiva de la compañía ha comenzado a cambiar la manera en que hacemos las cosas en esta sede, y **los departamentos han sido reorganizados** de ciertas formas. **Algunos cargos se han cambiado o eliminado por completo.**

June: Entiendo... Bueno, ahora me siento un poco preocupada. ¿De qué vamos a hablar acá?

Harry: El día de ayer recibí un correo electrónico de parte de mis superiores, en el cual **ilustraban, de manera detallada y específica,** los cambios a realizarse en esta sede, incluyendo una lista de los cargos que serían eliminados, además de **las personas de las que vamos a prescindir.**

June: Oh, ya sé de qué trata esta conversación.

Harry: Sí, June. **Lamentándolo mucho, debo informarte que no vamos a requerir tus servicios a partir del final de este mes,** ya que **tu cargo ha sido fusionado con el de supervisor** de atención al cliente, el cual será llenado por **un especialista de la capital.** El aviso te llega el día de hoy para que tengas tiempo de **arreglar tus asuntos** y buscar un nuevo empleo en el mercado. Como **agradecimiento,** incluiremos **un bono en tu indemnización** por despido.

June: Eso no es lo que quisiera, —me encantaría mantener mi trabajo, sin importar si es en algún departamento nuevo con otro cargo—. He dedicado siete años de mi vida a esta empresa y **creo que nunca he fallado en mis responsabilidades. Me gustaría que reconsideraran esta**

decisión, ya que he sido una trabajadora eficiente y dedicada.

Harry: **Mil disculpas**, June, pero la decisión es final. Me duele mucho tener que darte esta noticia, además de haberla recibido; la verdad es que **estás entre mis mejores empleados** y eres una de las personas que más ha generado resultados para esta sede. Lamentablemente, **no soy el que decide ni el que da la orden**, y lo máximo que puedo hacer por ti es **brindarte una recomendación para tus futuros empleos.**

June: Esto no puede estar pasando, señor Harry. **Actualmente debo cubrir los gastos de mi hogar** y, con esta **crisis de desempleo**, no será fácil encontrar otro trabajo. **Probablemente me mantenga desempleada** por un largo tiempo.

Harry: Podrías probar con los **beneficios del estado para desempleados**, recuerda que existe esa opción.

June: No podré calificar para esos beneficios, ya que **poseo una vivienda y automóvil propio**, y eso hace que esté en **baja prioridad**. Realmente necesito que lo reconsidere, señor Harry.

Harry: No es posible, June. Ya la decisión fue tomada. Ahora bien, voy a intentar lograr una extensión de emergencia a tu contrato hasta septiembre, es lo máximo que me darán. Jamás lo he tenido que hacer antes, pero lo haré por consideración a ti y a tus hijos. ¿Qué tal suena eso? Les recordaré todo lo que has aportado para la empresa y pediré que el nuevo cargo **entre en efecto** para el primero de octubre.

June: ¿En serio haría eso? ¡No se imagina cuán agradecida estoy al saberlo! No sería fácil para mí llegar a casa hoy y **decirles a mis hijos que fui despedida** y que pronto no tendré dinero para cubrir los gastos. Esto mejora un poco mi situación, ya que me da tiempo suficiente para hallar nuevas oportunidades. **¡Ha salvado a mi familia!**

Harry: No te preocupes, en serio, es una forma de agradecerte a ti por tus servicios y los resultados que has producido para nosotros a lo largo de los años. Déjame escribir ese correo electrónico ya, antes de que envíen al nuevo trabajador. Esto ha sido todo. Lamento darte esa noticia, pero **sé que podrás recuperar tu camino**. Recuerda también que voy a recomendarte.

June: Sí, señor Harry. **Todas las historias deben llegar a su fin**. Gracias por tenerme trabajando en esta empresa. **Nunca lo olvidaré**. Regresaré a mi puesto a seguir trabajando.

English

June: Good morning, Mr. Harry, how are you? **I'm sorry for arriving a bit late to the appointment,** I was finishing some tasks at the office. I was informed this morning that you needed to see me.

Harry: Yes, June. Thanks for coming and don't worry. Take a seat. That's true, **I needed to inform you of something.**

June: Let's see, what might it be? **Is it something serious? I feel the tension in the atmosphere,** to be honest.

Harry: Well, June, it's important that we talk a bit about the company and the **restructuring** that is being carried out at this moment in time. The company's board has begun to change the way in which we do things at this branch, and **the departments have been reorganized** in certain ways. **Some positions have been changed or eliminated entirely.**

June: I understand... Okay, and now I feel a bit worried. What are we going to talk about here?

Harry: Yesterday, I received an email from my superiors, in which they **illustrated, specifically and in detail,** the changes to be made at this branch, including a list of the positions that would be eliminated, **as well as the people we are going to lay off.**

June: Oh, I know what this conversation is about now.

Harry: Yes, June. **With great regret, I must inform you that we are no longer going to require your services starting from the end of this month,** since **your position has been merged with that of the customer service supervisor,** which will be filled by **a specialist from the capital.** The notice arrives today for you to have time to **arrange your affairs** and find a new job in the market. As **appreciation,** we will include **a bonus in your severance pay.**

June: That's not really what I want – I would love to keep my job, without caring if it's in a new department with another position. I've dedicated seven years of my life to this company, and **I believe I've never failed in my responsibilities. I would like for this decision to be reconsidered,** because I have been a faithful and efficient worker.

Harry: I beg forgiveness, June, but the decision is final. It hurts a lot for me to have to give you this news, as well as having received it; the truth is that **you are among my best employees** and are also one of the people who has generated results for this branch. Unfortunately, **I'm not the one who decides or gives the order**, and the best I can do for you is **provide you a recommendation for your future jobs**.

June: This can't be happening, Mr. Harry. **I currently have to cover the expenses at home**, and with this **unemployment crisis** it won't be easy to find another job. **I will probably stay unemployed** for a long time.

Harry: You could try the **state benefits for the unemployed**, remember that the option exists.

June: **I won't qualify for those benefits**, because **I own a home and car**, and that makes me a **low priority** person. I really need you to reconsider, Mr. Harry.

Harry: It isn't possible, June. The decision has been made. Now, I'm going to try to get an emergency extension of your contract until September, which is the most I can get. I've never had to do it before, but I will in consideration of your kids and yourself. How does that sound? I'll remind them of everything you've provided for the company and will ask that the new position **comes into effect** on the first of October.

June: Would you really do that for me? You can't imagine how thankful I am to know it! It wouldn't be easy to arrive home today and **tell my kids I've been fired** and that soon I won't have money to cover the expenses. This slightly improves my situation, since it gives me enough time to find new opportunities. **You've saved my family!**

Harry: Don't worry, seriously, it's a way of thanking you for your services and the results you've produced for us throughout the years. Let me write this email now, before they send the new worker. This has been all. I apologize for giving you that news, but **I know you'll be able to get back on your path**. Also remember that I'll be recommending you.

June: Yes, Mr. Harry. **All stories must reach their ending.** Thank you for having me work for this company. **I'll never forget you.** I'll go back to my working station to continue working.

CHAPTER 20

SOLVING WORK CONFLICTS

¡ES POR LAS BUENAS O POR LAS MALAS! – IT'S EITHER THE EASY WAY OR THE HARD WAY!

Vocabulary List

- **he escuchado de parte de tu supervisor** = I've heard on your supervisor's behalf
- **actualmente existe un problema algo grave dentro de tu departamento** = there is a serious problem currently going on in your department
- **¿podrías comunicármelo en tus propias palabras?** = could you explain it to me in your own words?
- **pienso que lo mejor es retirarme de esta empresa** = I believe that the best thing to do is to resign from this company
- **un descontento muy grande** = a very large discontent
- **no puedo trabajar en un ambiente así** = I can't work in an environment like this
- **vamos a tomarlo con calma** = let's take it easy.
- **¿tiene idea del acoso laboral al que he sido sujeta?** = do you have any idea of the workplace harassment I've been a victim of?
- **conozco muy poco de este caso** = I know very little about this case
- **me transmitas el problema** = transmit the problem to me
- **es mejor que hablemos con calma y con detalles** = it's best that we talk calmly and with many details
- **después de haber entendido todos los pormenores de este asunto** = after all of the subject's specifics have been understood
- **están haciéndome sentir como si fuera menos que ellos** = who are making me feel as if I am much less than them

158

- **haciendo comentarios sobre mi desempeño, mi apariencia y otras cualidades o defectos** = making comments every day about my performance, my appearance and other qualities and defects
- **¡he reportado numerosas veces este problema al supervisor y no he logrado nada!** = **I've reported this problem numerous times to the supervisor and have accomplished nothing!**
- **¿has intentado hablar con alguien aparte de...?** = ¿have you attempted to speak with anyone besides...?
- **¡cinco de los peores meses de mi vida!** = five of the worst months of my life!
- **me aseguraré de ir directamente al Ministerio de Trabajo a reportar a la empresa** = I'll make sure to go straight to the Work Ministry to report the company
- **sí tendrán que tomar cartas en el asunto** = you will all have to address the issue then
- **no será bonito para la directiva cuando tengan acá a los empleados del Ministerio!** = it won't be pretty for the board when they have Minister employees here!
- **no te voy a mentir** = I'm not going to lie to you
- **amonestar e incluso suspender a los empleados que están causándote problemas** = warn and even suspend the employees that are causing you trouble
- **¿estarías dispuesta a brindar una declaración grabada y escrita?** = would you be willing to take a recorded and written statement?
- **un par de testigos** = a couple of witnesses
- **¡involucraré una demanda en esto!** = involve a lawsuit in this!
- **llamaré al abogado de la empresa y comenzaremos con la declaración** = I'll call the company's lawyer and we can begin with the statement
- **de manera confidencial** = confidentially
- **sí necesito que sean amonestados, suspendidos y reasignados** = I do need them to be warned, suspended and reassigne
- **es mi exigencia, y espero que sea respetada.** = it's my demand, and I hope that it is respected
- **estoy de acuerdo en que es una exigencia justa** = I'm in

agreement that it is a fair demand

- **fracasó en darle una respuesta rápida a tu problema** = failed in providing a quick response to your problem
- **no es sano para nadie** = it isn't healthy for anybody
- **parece que resolveré por fin esta situación** = it seems that I'm finally going to resolve this situation
- **te lo presento** = I introduce you to him

Spanish

Sergio: Hola, Sofía, gracias por asistir a mi oficina y, por supuesto, por entender que era necesario que pasaras por acá. **He escuchado de parte de tu supervisor** que **actualmente existe un problema algo grave dentro de tu departamento. ¿Podrías comunicármelo en tus propias palabras?**

Sofía: Buenas tardes, señor Sergio, sí: hay un grave problema ocurriendo en estos momentos. **Pienso que lo mejor es retirarme de esta empresa** y no mirar hacia atrás nuevamente. Esta situación está causándome estrés, problemas en casa y **un descontento muy grande. No puedo trabajar en un ambiente así.**

Sergio: A ver, Sofía, **vamos a tomarlo con calma.**

Sofía: ¿Con calma? **¿Tiene idea del acoso laboral al que he sido sujeta** en los últimos meses?

Sergio: Conozco muy poco de este caso, pero estoy tratando de que **me transmitas el problema. Es mejor que hablemos con calma y con detalles.** Se podrá tomar una decisión **después de haber entendido todos los pormenores de este asunto.** A ver, ¿qué está ocurriendo?

Sofía: Tengo una serie de hostigadores en mi oficina, quienes **están haciéndome sentir como si fuera menos que ellos**, todos los días **haciendo comentarios sobre mi desempeño, mi apariencia y otras cualidades o defectos** que tengo. **¡He reportado numerosas veces este problema al supervisor y no he logrado nada!**

Sergio: Eso es grave, Sofía. **¿Has intentado hablar con alguien aparte de tu supervisor?** ¿Desde cuándo está ocurriendo este problema?

Sofía: La verdad es que desde el pasado mes de agosto, es decir, ¡cinco meses! **¡Cinco de los peores meses de mi vida!** Pero lo peor no es lo que ha sucedido, sino que eres la tercera persona con la que trato de hablar, ¡y no ha cambiado nada! Si renuncio, **me aseguraré de ir directamente al Ministerio de Trabajo a reportar a la empresa.** Creo que ahí **sí tendrán que tomar cartas en el asunto,** pero **¡no será bonito para la directiva cuando tengan acá a los empleados del Ministerio!**

Sergio: Sí, Sofía. Entiendo. **No te voy a mentir** —hemos estado en esa situación antes y de verdad quiero hacer todo lo posible por no estarlo nuevamente–. Lo mejor para resolver esto sería **amonestar e incluso suspender a los empleados que están causándote problemas. ¿Estarías dispuesta brindar una declaración grabada y escrita?** Es la mejor manera de que quede en evidencia lo que estás contándome.

Sofía: Estoy dispuesta a hacer eso y todo lo que sea necesario. Puedo dar todos sus nombres y tengo **un par de testigos** que han decidido ayudarme con esta situación. Pero, le advierto, este es mi último intento por arreglar las cosas por las buenas. Si no funciona, ¡prometo que iré al Ministerio e **involucraré una demanda en esto!**

Sergio: Eso no será necesario. Vamos, **llamaré al abogado de la empresa y comenzaremos con la declaración.** ¿Hay algo que desees contarme **de manera confidencial** antes de que llegue?

Sofía: Sí. La verdad es que no quisiera que despidan a estos trabajadores. Sé que tampoco la están pasando bien, debido a la presión que todos tenemos encima ahorita por las ventas del segundo trimestre del año, pero **sí necesito que sean amonestados, suspendidos y reasignados. Es mi exigencia, y espero que sea respetada.**

Sergio: Sí, **estoy de acuerdo en que es una exigencia justa.** No tengo nada que decirte sobre lo que pides, ya que es totalmente respetable. Quizá la empresa **fracasó en darle una respuesta rápida a tu problema**, y por eso hemos llegado hasta acá. Me aseguraré de que tu supervisor sea informado de que ha cometido una grave falta. Este tipo de circunstancias jamás deben ser ignoradas. **No es sano para nadie.**

Sofía: Gracias, señor. Sabía que, al menos con usted, iba a lograr algo. Y **parece que resolveré por fin esta situación.** Me ha gustado trabajar aquí y no quisiera irme.

Sergio: Ni tendrás que hacerlo. Bueno, ya está aquí el abogado de la empresa. **Te lo presento.** Ahora, ¡comencemos!

English

Sergio: Hello Sofia, thank you for coming to my office and, of course, for understanding that it was necessary for you to come by here. **I've heard on your supervisor's behalf** that **there is a serious problem currently going on in your department. Could you explain it to me in your own words?**

Sofia: Good afternoon, Mr. Sergio, yes – there is a major problem taking place at present. **I believe that the best thing to do is to resign from this company** and not look back again. This situation is causing me stress, problems at home and **a very large discontent. I can't work in an environment like this.**

Sergio: Let's see, Sofia, **let's take it easy.**

Sofia: Take it easy? **Do you have any idea of the workplace harassment I've been a victim of** during the last few months?

Sergio: I know very little about this case, but I'm attempting for you to **transmit the problem to me. It's best that we talk calmly and with many details.** A decision will be made **after all of the subject's specifics have been understood.** Very well, so what is going on?

Sofia: I have a number of bullies in my office, **who are making me feel as if I am much less than them, making comments every day about my performance, my appearance and other qualities and defects that I possess. I've reported this problem numerous times to the supervisor and have accomplished nothing!**

Sergio: That is serious, Sofia. **¿Have you attempted to speak with anyone besides** your supervisor? For how long exactly has this problem been occurring?

Sofia: The truth is that since last August, in other words, five months! **Five of the worst months of my life!** But the worst part isn't what has happened, but the fact that you're the third person I attempt to talk to, and nothing has changed at all! If I quit, **I'll make sure to go straight to the Work Ministry to report the company.** I believe that **you will all have to address the issue then,** but **it won't be pretty for the board when they**

have Minister employees here!

Sergio: Yes, Sofia. I understand. **I'm not going to lie to you** – we have been in this situation before, and I truly want to do as much as I can to avoid being in it again. The best thing to do to resolve this is to **warn and even suspend the employees that are causing you trouble. Would you be willing to take a recorded and written statement?** It's the best way to keep evidence of what you're telling me.

Sofia: I am willing to do all of that and everything else that may be necessary. I can give you all the names, and I have **a couple of witnesses** who have decided to help me out with this situation. But I warn you, this is my last attempt to fix things the easy way. If it doesn't work, I promise I will go to the Ministry and **involve a lawsuit in this!**

Sergio: That won't be necessary. Come on, **I'll call the company's lawyer and we can begin with the statement.** Anything else you wish to tell me **confidentially** before he arrives?

Sofia: Yes. The truth is that I wouldn't want the employees to be fired. I know they're not having an easy time either due to the pressure we're all suffering from right now because of the second quarter of the year sales, but **I do need them to be warned, suspended and reassigned. It's my demand, and I hope that it is respected.**

Sergio: Yeah, **I'm in agreement that it is a fair demand.** I don't have anything to say about what you're asking for, since it is totally respectable. Perhaps the company **failed in providing a quick response to your problem**, and that is why we've come to this point. I will make sure that your supervisor is informed that he has committed a serious fault. This type of circumstance must never be ignored. **It isn't healthy for anybody.**

Sofia: Thank you, sir. I knew that at least with you I would accomplish something. And **it seems that I'm finally going to resolve this situation.** I've always liked working here, and wouldn't want to leave.

Sergio: Nor will you have to. Okay, the company's lawyer is here now. **I introduce you to him.** Fine, let's begin!

CHAPTER 21

CHARGING WHAT YOU'RE OWED

VAMOS, ¡NECESITO EL DINERO! – COME ON, I NEED THE MONEY!

Vocabulary List

- **no me había puesto en contacto contigo** = I hadn't gotten in contact with you
- **estresarte la vida** = stress out
- **yo ya le entregué el sitio web a un representante de tu empresa hace diez días** = I already handed over the website to a representative of your company ten days ago
- **nunca recibí respuesta** = I never received a response
- **las obligaciones del negocio** = the company obligations
- **me quitan todo el tiempo para responder** = take all the time that I could spend on answering
- **¿vienes buscando otro trabajo parecido?** = are you looking for another similar task?
- **vengo a cobrar por el sitio web que ya les creé** = I'm here to charge for the website that I created for you
- **solicité el pago por ese trabajo hace ya diez días, cuando entregué los resultados** = I requested a payment for that project ten days ago when I submitted the results
- **hasta el día de hoy no he recibido nada** = until today I haven't received anything
- **¿cómo puede haber ocurrido esto?** = how could that have happened?
- **acordé trabajar con ustedes sin un anticipo** = I agreed to work with you guys without a retainer
- **cuando me respondieron, rápidamente me colgaron, como para**

165

no perder el tiempo conmigo = when the phone was answered, it was quickly hung up as if to not waste time with me

- **no vayas a pensar que te estamos evadiendo** =_don't start thinking we're avoiding you

- **no cobré por adelantado** = I didn't bill you in advance

- **se ha vuelto bastante difícil recibir el pago que me gané con trabajo y resultados** = it has become very difficult to receive the payment which I earned with my work and results

- **puede ser bien difícil trabajar sin que te paguen lo que te deben** = it can be quite difficult to work without being paid what you're owed

- **enviar a alguien detrás de ellos para exigirles el pago** = send someone after them so that we can demand payment

- **no evitamos pagarte de ninguna manera** = we haven't avoided paying you at all

- **yo ni siquiera sabía que no te habían pagado** = I didn't even know you hadn't been paid

- **yo te escribí por correo electrónico durante varios días** = I attempted to contact you through email for several days

- **dejé un recado con tu secretaria** = leaving you a message with your secretary

- **acá estoy, el día de hoy, reclamando mi pago** = here I am today demanding my payment

- **sé que te debemos** = I know we owe it to you

- **haré unas transferencias hoy en la noche a varios proveedores** = I'll do some transfers today, to several suppliers

- **no voy a esperar a que me pagues esta noche** = I'm not going to wait to be paid tonight

- **yo necesito el dinero** = I need the money

- **¿en dónde quedó la confianza?** = what happened with our trust?

- **pensé que nuestra palabra valía cuando se trataba de nuestra amistad** = I thought our word was our bond when it came to our friendship

- **la verdad es que me estás evadiendo** = the truth is that you're evading me

166

- **difamación** = slander
- **es lamentable que ahora nuestra confianza quede dañada para siempre** = it's unfortunate that now our trust will be damaged forever
- **a nadie le gusta que le deban, ni a ti** = nobody likes being owed, not even you

Spanish

Ricardo: ¡Oh, Tati! ¿Cómo estás? Imagino que ya tienes el diseño del sitio web creado y todo. **No me había puesto en contacto contigo** para dejarte trabajar tranquila en tu departamento y no **estresarte la vida** con mis comentarios. Así que... ¿cuándo voy a mirar tu trabajo?

Tatiana: Ehh, sí, hola, Ricardo. La verdad es que **yo ya le entregué el sitio web a un representante de tu empresa hace diez días.** Lo finalicé hace dos semanas y me puse en contacto contigo, pero **nunca recibí respuesta.**

Ricardo: Entiendo, ¡lo siento mucho! Ya sabes, **las obligaciones del negocio** que **me quitan todo el tiempo para responder.**

Tatiana: Sí, supongo que eso ocurre cuando estás a cargo de una empresa como esta.

Ricardo: Exactamente. Bueno, entonces, ¿qué es lo que te trae aquí el día de hoy? **¿Vienes buscando otro trabajo parecido?** Puede que tengamos algo, ya que estamos expandiéndonos a otras geografías y en otros idiomas...

Tatiana: Eso sería interesante, Ricardo, pero la verdad es que no, no vengo por trabajo. **Vengo a cobrar por el sitio web que ya les creé; solicité el pago por ese trabajo hace ya diez días, cuando entregué los resultados,** y **hasta el día de hoy no he recibido nada.**

Ricardo: ¿Qué? ¡Imposible! **¿Cómo puede haber ocurrido esto?** No lo puedo creer.

Tatiana: Pues sí, Ricardo, sí ocurrió. **Acordé trabajar con ustedes sin un anticipo** porque hay confianza entre tú y yo, pero esta situación no me ha gustado nada. He llamado por teléfono todos los días y nadie me responde. **Cuando me respondieron, rápidamente me colgaron, como para no perder el tiempo conmigo.**

Ricardo: Eso puede haber sido un problema de las líneas telefónicas, o simplemente no había alguien disponible para tomar tu llamada. **No vayas a pensar que te estamos evadiendo** o algo así.

Tatiana: La verdad es que así parece. Como te dije, **no cobré por adelantado** y ahora **se ha vuelto bastante difícil recibir el pago que me gané con trabajo y resultados.**

Ricardo: Sí, imagino que **puede ser bien difícil trabajar sin que te paguen lo que te deben.** Algunas veces me ha sucedido que un cliente trata de hacernos eso, pero debemos **enviar a alguien detrás de ellos para exigirles el pago.**

Tatiana: Algo así como lo que estoy haciendo yo hoy, ¿no?

Ricardo: No, no. Nada parecido. **No evitamos pagarte de ninguna manera,** Tati. No pienses mal, por favor. **Yo ni siquiera sabía que no te habían pagado.**

Tatiana: Lo que sucede es que **yo te escribí por correo electrónico durante varios días,** además de que **dejé un recado con tu secretaria.** Es por eso que no entiendo cómo dices que no sabías. Es todo un poco extraño, pero **acá estoy, el día de hoy, reclamando mi pago.**

Ricardo: **Sé que te debemos,** pero se te hará llegar. **Haré unas transferencias hoy en la noche a varios proveedores:** tu pago estará entre ellos. Muchas gracias por todos tus servicios y por la espera, Tati.

Tatiana: No, Ricardo. **No voy a esperar a que me pagues esta noche.** He estado esperando por diez días desde que entregué el sitio web. **Yo necesito el dinero,** tengo dos hijos pequeños y están en la escuela. Tampoco quiero explicaciones. Solo necesito mi dinero y ya.

Ricardo: **¿En dónde quedó la confianza, Tatiana? Pensé que nuestra palabra valía cuando se trataba de nuestra amistad.**

Tatiana: Yo también lo pensaba, pero claramente no es así. **La verdad es que me estás evadiendo,** lo cual no solo es deshonesto, sino que también es irresponsable. Imagínate que yo le dijera a mis conocidos que no te gusta pagar por los trabajos grandes que solicitas: sería problemático para ti.

Ricardo: ¿Acaso me estás amenazando, Tatiana? Eso es **difamación,** creo que no te iría nada bien si haces eso. Tranquila, **haré el pago ahora mismo para que cerremos este problema.**

Tatiana: Así mismo me gusta, Ricardo. **Es lamentable que ahora nuestra confianza quede dañada para siempre. A nadie le gusta que le deban, ni a ti.** Espero tomes esto en cuenta para el futuro. Te lo digo como amiga.

English

Ricardo: Oh Tati, how are you doing? I'm guessing you now have the website design done and dusted. **I hadn't gotten in contact with you** so that you could work in peace in your department and not **stress out** with my comments. So... when am I going to be able to take a look at your work?

Tatiana: Uhh, yeah, hello, Ricardo. The truth is that **I already handed over the website to a representative of your company ten days ago.** I finished it two weeks ago and tried to contact you, but **never received a response.**

Ricardo: I understand, forgive me! You know, **the company obligations** that **take all the time that I could spend on answering.**

Tatiana: Yes, I'm guessing that happens when you're in charge of a company such as this one.

Ricardo: Exactly. Well, what was it that made you come here today? **Are you looking for another similar task?** We may have something available, since we're expanding to new geographical regions and languages...

Tatiana: That would be interesting, Ricardo, but the truth is that no, I'm not here for work. **I'm here to charge for the website that I created for you; I requested a payment for that project ten days ago when I submitted the results,** and **until today I haven't received anything.**

Ricardo: What? Impossible! **How could that have happened?** I can't believe it.

Tatiana: Well actually, Ricardo, it did happen. **I agreed to work with you guys without a retainer** because of the trust between us both, but I haven't enjoyed this situation at all. I've called by phone every single day, and nobody answers. **When the phone was answered, it was quickly hung up as if to not waste time with me.**

Ricardo: That might have been a problem with the line, or simply there wasn't anyone available to take your call. **Don't start thinking we're avoiding you** or something similar.

Tatiana: The truth is that it seems that way. As I said, **I didn't bill you in advance,** and now **it has become very difficult to receive the payment**

which I earned with my work and results.

Ricardo: Yes, I imagine **it can be quite difficult to work without being paid what you're owed**. Sometimes it has happened to me that a client attempts to do that, but we must **send someone after them so that we can demand payment**.

Tatiana: Something like what I'm doing here today, correct?

Ricardo: No, no. Nothing of the sort. **We haven't avoided paying you at all**, Tati. Don't think badly of us, please. **I didn't even know you hadn't been paid**.

Tatiana: What is going on is that I that **I attempted to contact you through email for several days**, as well as **leaving you a message with your secretary**. That is why I don't understand why you're saying you weren't aware. It's all a bit strange, but **here I am today demanding my payment**.

Ricardo: **I know we owe it to you**, but we'll have it sent over. **I'll do some transfers today, to several suppliers** – your payment will be among them. Thank you for all of your services and for the wait, Tati.

Tatiana: No, Ricardo. **I'm not going to wait to be paid tonight**. I have been waiting for ten days since I submitted the website. **I need the money**; I have two small children and they're at school. I don't want any explanations, either. I just need my money and that's it.

Ricardo: **What happened with our trust**, Tatiana? **I thought our word was our bond when it came to our friendship.**

Tatiana: I also believed it, but it's clearly not like that. **The truth is that you're evading me**, which isn't just dishonest, but also irresponsible. Imagine I told my acquaintances that you were accustomed to not paying for the larger jobs you request – that would be a problem for you.

Ricardo: Are you threatening me, Tatiana? That's **slander**, and I think it wouldn't go well for you if you did that. Don't worry, I will make the payment right now so that we can end this problem.

Tatiana: That's the way I like it, Ricardo. **It's unfortunate that now our trust will be damaged forever. Nobody likes being owed, not even you.** I hope you take this into account for the future. I'm telling you as a friend.

CHAPTER 22

RENTING OFFICE SPACE

¡ESTE SERÁ EL LUGAR PERFECTO PARA TU NEGOCIO! – THIS WILL BE THE PERFECT PLACE FOR YOUR BUSINESS!

Vocabulary List

- **¿tuvo problemas en ubicar este lugar?** = did you have trouble finding this place?
- **fue un poco problemático encontrar el lugar** = it was a bit troublesome to find this place
- **la vista lo vale todo** = the view is worth it
- **una de las zonas más exclusivas del país** = one of the most exclusive areas in the country
- **no tiene que lidiar con el tráfico, el ruido, la delincuencia** = doesn't have to deal with traffic, noise, petty crime
- **todos los exteriores de estos edificios** = the exteriors of these buildings
- **buenas vistas** = great views
- **productividad propia y de los empleados** = personal productivity and that of your employees
- **especies de flora y fauna únicas** = unique species of flora and fauna
- **techo** = roof
- **disfrutar de sus amaneceres y atardeceres** = enjoy dawn and dusk
- **espacios exteriores vistosos** = eye-catching exterior spaces
- **mejor ética de trabajo** = better work ethic
- **ayudar a incrementar los lazos entre el empleado y la empresa** = help increase the bonds between the employee and the company

- **la arquitectura del sitio** = architecture of the place
- **firma personal de nuestro arquitecto favorito** = personal signature of our own favorite architect
- **obra de arte** = work of art
- **socios** = associates
- **llevar a cabo reuniones** = start meetings
- **deslumbrarían** = dazzle
- **parte de aquí afuera** = outside area
- **la entrada al edificio** = the building's entrance
- **puertas de madera tropical de merbau** = tropical merbau wooden doors
- **importadas** = imported
- **los pasillos** = the corridors
- **roble europeo y mármol** = European oak and of marble
- **las oficinas de planta baja** = ground floor offices
- **son bastante espaciosas** = they're quite spacious
- **perfectas para permitir la movilidad de los empleados** = perfect to allow mobility among employees
- **odian estar encerrados en cubículos** = hate being enclosed in cubicles
- **estas oficinas les permitirán moverse de un lado a otro** = these offices will enable them to move from one place to another
- **no puedo ver cables por ninguna parte** = I can't see cables anywhere
- **también me encantan las vistas** = I also love the views
- **cada oficina tiene sus detalles distintos** = each office has its different details
- **su coloración** = its colors
- **sala de reuniones** = meeting room
- **enorme** = enormous
- **mucha luz natural** = plenty of natural light
- **acústica** = acoustics
- **puertos USB, LAN y WiFi** = USB, LAN and WiFi ports
- **todas sus necesidades de internet y conectividad** = your internet

and connectivity needs

- **ventanas panorámicas** = panoramic windows
- **una vista a la ciudad en el fondo** = a view towards the city in the background
- **la planta alta** = the top floor
- **¿cuánto me costará?** = how much will it cost me?
- **quiero alquilar este sitio** = I want to rent this place
- **vamos a firmar ese contrato** = get to signing that contract
- **¡voy a tener la mejor oficina de la industria entera!** = I'm going to have the best office in the whole industry!

Spanish

Naomi: Oh, hola, señor Magnus. ¡Estoy tan feliz de que esté acá! **¿Tuvo problemas en ubicar este lugar?** Sé que requiere un poco de búsqueda.

Magnus: ¡Hola, Naomi! Sí, pues, **fue un poco problemático encontrar el lugar,** pero **la vista lo vale todo.** Digo, ¡vaya!, ¡hay unos edificios bastante hermosos en esta zona!

Naomi: ¡Definitivamente! Esta zona es en realidad **una de las zonas más exclusivas del país,** y una que **no tiene que lidiar con el tráfico, el ruido, la delincuencia** o cualquiera de todos esos otros problemas que traen las grandes ciudades consigo. Así que, hoy comenzaré enseñándole **todos los exteriores de estos edificios** porque, créame: va a querer mirar todo lo que puede disfrutar *afuera* de su nueva oficina antes de entrar.

Magnus: ¿Es en serio? Perfecto, entonces, —de todas maneras, soy alguien a quien le encantan la naturaleza y las **buenas vistas**—. Un buen ambiente también es perfecto para mejorar la **productividad propia y de los empleados.** ¡Comencemos, entonces!

Naomi: ¡Excelente! Lo primero que debe saber es que esta zona es una de las pocas donde podrá encontrar **especies de flora y fauna únicas,** como estas palmas carnauba que solo crecen en Brasil y esos loros que podrá observar en el **techo** de aquella estructura. Realmente podrá **disfrutar de sus amaneceres y atardeceres** mirando los preciosos animales que salen a comer y tomar agua a esas horas. ¿Qué le parece?

Magnus: Eso es algo realmente genial para encontrar en tal lugar, bastante raro, de hecho. Se ha probado en estudios importantes que los **espacios exteriores vistosos** pueden llevar a una **mejor ética de trabajo** y **ayudar a incrementar los lazos entre el empleado y la empresa** para la que trabaja, ya que se sienten agradecidos con sus alrededores. También estoy observando que **la arquitectura del sitio** es bastante impresionante. Todo pareciera hecho por alguien con buen gusto.

Naomi: Como podrá imaginar, la estructura tiene la **firma personal de nuestro arquitecto favorito,** García. ¿Lo conoce? Sí, aunque no lo crea, esta estructura fue creada por el mismísimo ganador del premio

Arquitecto del Año. Es más una **obra de arte** que un simple edificio. Sería excelente para que usted y su empresa trajeran a sus **socios** a hablar aquí y **llevar a cabo reuniones**, las cuales **deslumbrarían** a todos sin que hayan entrado siquiera. Dará mucho de qué hablar.

Magnus: Perfecto, ciertamente estoy convencido con esta **parte de aquí afuera**. Ahora, entremos y veamos qué hay de interesante. Si es así por fuera, por dentro debe ser hermosísimo.

Naomi: ¡Eso definitivamente es cierto, señor Magnus! No falla su lógica en esa parte. Si le ha gustado lo que ha visto hasta ahora, no tiene idea de lo increíble que será lo que falta por ver. Ahora, comencemos por **la entrada al edificio: puertas de madera tropical de merbau, importadas** desde Indonesia para ser instaladas acá. **Los pasillos** de la mayor parte del edificio son de **roble europeo y mármol**, pero no permita que eso lo intimide. Realmente, estamos hablando de calidad por lo que está pagando, y acá ofrecemos los mayores niveles en calidad.

Magnus: Todo esto es precioso – ahora pasemos a **las oficinas de planta baja**. Vaya, veo que **son bastante espaciosas, perfectas para permitir la movilidad de los empleados.** Muchos **odian estar encerrados en cubículos**, y **estas oficinas les permitirán moverse de un lado a otro.** Además, noto que **no puedo ver cables por ninguna parte.** Es muy discreto. **También me encantan las vistas** que pueden observarse desde cada ventana. Y, ¿esta otra oficina? Interesante, no es exactamente igual a la otra.

Naomi: ¡Es así! **Cada oficina tiene sus detalles distintos**, incluso en **su coloración**, aunque es sutil. Vayamos ahora a la **sala de reuniones**... Como verá, es **enorme**, con **mucha luz natural** para crear un ambiente agradable para los invitados. La **acústica** también es perfecta, y hay **puertos USB, LAN y WiFi** para **todas sus necesidades de internet y conectividad**. Lo mejor de todo es que tiene **ventanas panorámicas** con **una vista a la ciudad en el fondo**, como podrá observar. Realmente, es otro nivel de lujo en lo que a salas de reunión se refiere. Apuesto a que nunca había visto algo parecido.

Magnus: Créame que no. Ahora, antes de subir a **la planta alta** y terminar de ver todo lo impresionante que es este lugar, tengo la pregunta más importante de todas... **¿cuánto me costará?** Estoy convencido. **Quiero alquilar este sitio**, así que hablemos de costos y **vamos a firmar ese contrato. ¡Voy a tener la mejor oficina de la industria entera!**

English

Naomi: Well, hello there, Mr. Magnus. I'm so glad that you're here! **Did you have trouble finding this place?** I know it requires a bit of searching.

Magnus: Hello Naomi! Yes, **it was a bit troublesome to find this place,** but **the view is worth it.** I mean, wow, there are actually quite beautiful buildings out here!

Naomi: Definitely! This area is actually **one of the most exclusive areas in the country,** and one which **doesn't have to deal with traffic, noise, petty crime** or all of the other issues that the big cities bring with them. So, today I'll begin by showing you around **the exteriors of these buildings,** because believe me – you're going to want to see everything you can enjoy *outside* of your new office before you go in.

Magnus: Is that true? Perfect, then – in any case I'm someone who loves nature and **great views.** An excellent atmosphere is also perfect to improve your **personal productivity and that of your employees.** Let's start, then!

Naomi: Excellent! The first thing you must know is that this area is one of the only places where you can find **unique species of flora and fauna,** such as these Carnauba palms which only grow in Brazil, and those parrots you can observe on the **roof** of that structure. You'll really be able to **enjoy dawn and dusk** watching these precious animals that come out to eat and drink water at these times. What do you think?

Magnus: That is quite a wonderful thing to encounter in such a place, quite rare in fact. It has been proven in important studies that **eye-catching exterior spaces** can lead to a **better work ethic** and **help increase the bonds between the employee and the company** they are working for, as they feel grateful with their surroundings. I'm also observing that the **architecture of the place** is quite impressive. It all looks like it was made by somebody with good taste.

Naomi: As you may imagine, the structure has the **personal signature of our own favorite architect,** Garcia. Do you know him? Yes, believe it or not, this structure was created by the winner of the Architect of the Year award himself. It is more a **work of art** than a simple building. It would be excellent for you and your company to bring your **associates** here to talk and **start meetings**, which would **dazzle** them all without having even come inside. It will give them a lot to talk about.

Magnus: Fine, I'm certainly convinced with this **outside area**. Now, let's go inside and see what there is of interest. If it's like this on the outside, it must be really beautiful inside.

Naomi: That is definitely true, Mr. Magnus! Your logic isn't wrong in that aspect. If you like what you've seen until now, you have no idea in how incredible what you haven't seen yet will be. Now, let's begin with **the building's entrance: tropical merbau wooden doors, imported** from Indonesia to be fitted here. **The corridors** of most of the building are made of **European oak and of marble**, but don't allow that to intimidate you. We're really talking about quality for what you're paying, and here we offer the highest levels of quality.

Magnus: All of this is beautiful – now let's move along to the **ground floor offices**. Wow, I can see that **they're quite spacious, perfect to allow mobility among employees. Many hate being enclosed in cubicles**, and **these offices will enable them to move from one place to another**. Furthermore, I note that **I can't see cables anywhere**. Very discreet. **I also love the views** which can be observed from each window. And this other office? Interesting, it isn't exactly the same as the other.

Naomi: That's precisely it! **Each office has its different details**, even in **its colors**, although it's subtle. Let's go now to the **meeting room**... As you may see, it is **enormous**, with **plenty of natural light** to create a pleasant atmosphere for the guests. The **acoustics** are perfect too, and there are **USB, LAN and WiFi ports** for all of **your internet and connectivity needs**. The best of it all is that it has **panoramic windows** with **a view towards the city in the background**, as you may observe. It really is another level of luxury in meeting rooms. I bet you have never seen anything similar.

Magnus: Trust me, I haven't. Now, before going up to **the top floor** and seeing the rest of the impressive things in this place, I have the most important question of them all... **how much will it cost me?** I'm convinced. **I want to rent this place**, so let's talk about costs and **get to signing that contract. I'm going to have the best office in the whole industry!**

BONUS CHAPTER

PROJECT MANAGEMENT
TODO ESTÁ EN MIS MANOS –
EVERYTHING IS IN MY HANDS

Vocabulary List

- **quedas totalmente a cargo de las operaciones por tres meses =** you're fully in charge of operations for three months

- **me gustaría que hiciéramos un último repaso =** I would like us to make one last brief

- **lo que se espera de mí en este nuevo rol =** what is expected of me in this new role

- **he sido entrenada durante dos meses para este momento =** I've received training for two months for this moment

- **quiero asegurar todas las bases =** I want to cover all the bases

- **voy a necesitar que te encargues de la gestión del personal =** I'm going to need you to oversee personnel management

- **investigaciones, preselección y contratación =** research, screening and contracting

- **pagos semanales y el desempeño =** weekly payments and performance

- **las más altas prioridades =** the highest priorities

- **sistema de ventas =** sales system

- **manejo de nuestros clientes =** management of our clients

- **aplicaciones informáticas que usamos para el registro de nuestros aliados =** the software we use for the registry of our allies

- **los proveedores y la adquisición de materias primas =** the suppliers and the acquirement of raw material

- **recibir y atender a los encargados de traer nuestra materia prima** = receive and attend to the people in charge of bringing our raw material
- **ingredientes para el comedor de los trabajadores** = ingredients for the workers' mess hall
- **el agua potable para las oficinas** = the drinking water for the offices
- **los materiales de limpieza y todo lo referente al material de papelería** = the cleaning materials and everything related to stationary
- **bien anotado** = well noted
- **lo que concierne a esos bienes sin los que no puede funcionar la empresa** = in terms of those goods which are crucial for the company's operation
- **no tendrás que crear la publicidad ni nada por el estilo** = you wouldn't have to create the advertisements or anything similar
- **publicidad en televisión, radio o redes sociales** = the advertising on television, radio or on social media
- **también desarrollaré una estrategia para el mercadeo por correo electrónico** = I'll also develop an email marketing strategy
- **una de nuestras debilidades que puede ser exitosamente aprovechada** = one of our weaknesses which could be successfully harnessed
- **una audiencia allí con la que podemos conectarnos** = an audience there with which we can connect
- **la imagen de nuestra marca** = our brand's image
- **refrescar nuestro logo y el eslogan de la empresa** = refreshing our logo and the company slogan
- **logos minimalistas** = minimalist logos
- **para que llegue a más personas** = so that it can reach more people
- **estratega de relaciones públicas** = public relations strategist
- **patrocinantes útiles** = useful sponsors
- **grandes acuerdos comerciales** = great commercial deals

- **obsoleto** = obsolete
- **te daré una respuesta definitiva una vez haya regresado** = I'll give you a definite answer once I've come back
- **cuida la empresa como si fuera tuya** = take care of the company as if it were your own
- **que todo estará mejor que como lo dejé** = that everything will be better than I left it

Spanish

Kyle: Bueno, ha llegado el gran momento para tomar mis merecidas vacaciones y apartarme un poco de este gran negocio que me mantiene ocupado veinticuatro horas al día, siete días a la semana. Como ya habíamos discutido, **quedas totalmente a cargo de las operaciones por tres meses.** ¿Preparada?

Victoria: Sí, Kyle, definitivamente estoy lista. Aun así, **me gustaría que hiciéramos un último repaso** de **lo que se espera de mí en este nuevo rol. He sido entrenada durante dos meses para este momento,** pero **quiero asegurar todas las bases.**

Kyle: Es una buena iniciativa, no hay problema si quieres. A ver, comencemos. Entre tus responsabilidades más importantes, **voy a necesitar que te encargues de la gestión del personal.** Todo lo que incluya **investigaciones, preselección y contratación,** además de los **pagos semanales y el desempeño.**

Victoria: Entiendo, eso está bien. ¿Qué otra cosa está entre **las más altas prioridades?**

Kyle: Realmente debes tener claro lo que espero en cuanto a nuestro **sistema de ventas.** Quiero que te familiarices con nuestro personal en este departamento, con el proceso que utilizan para el **manejo de nuestros clientes,** además de las **aplicaciones informáticas que usamos para el registro de nuestros aliados.**

Victoria: Perfecto. También me habían mencionado algo sobre **los proveedores y la adquisición de materias primas,** ¿no?

Kyle: Está muy bien que lo nombres: debemos tener bien claro que será una de tus grandes responsabilidades **recibir y atender a los encargados de traer nuestra materia prima,** además de los recursos necesarios, como los **ingredientes para el comedor de los trabajadores, el agua potable para las oficinas, los materiales de limpieza y todo lo referente al material de papelería.** Esto fácilmente puede olvidarse, así que toma nota.

Victoria: Sí, me aseguraré de tener **bien anotado** todo **lo que concierne a**

esos bienes sin los que no puede funcionar la empresa. Me encantaría saber algo: ¿qué hay de la publicidad que tenemos en uso actualmente? ¿También estaré detrás de todo eso?

Kyle: La verdad es que sí, no tendrás que crear la publicidad ni nada por el estilo, pero sí asegurar que esté funcionando y siendo publicado en cada canal indicado, ya sea la publicidad en televisión, radio o redes sociales. Por favor, no pierdas de vista estos tres canales para la publicidad.

Victoria: No, Kyle. Te prometo que tendré mi atención sobre eso en todo momento. También desarrollaré una estrategia para el mercadeo por correo electrónico, ya que es una de nuestras debilidades que puede ser exitosamente aprovechada con suficientes ideas. Tenemos una audiencia allí con la que podemos conectarnos.

Kyle: Excelente sugerencia. A ver, ¿qué otra cosa puedes ofrecernos en este tiempo que estaré ausente?

Victoria: Pues, pienso que puedo trabajar en la imagen de nuestra marca y en las posibilidades de refrescar nuestro logo y el eslogan de la empresa. Están muy de moda los logos minimalistas, y siento que podría trabajar en la personalidad de nuestra compañía para que llegue a más personas que se sientan identificadas con ella. Tengo experiencia en esto, debido a trabajos anteriores donde era la estratega de relaciones públicas, y también puedo ubicar patrocinantes útiles con los que podríamos lograr grandes acuerdos comerciales.

Kyle: ¡Suena genial! Pienso que ya es hora de un cambio en ambas cosas, ya que estamos trabajando con el logo que diseñó mi padre para la empresa hace alrededor de treinta y cinco años, además de un logo que a veces me ha parecido obsoleto en estos tiempos. Plantea varias ideas y yo te daré una respuesta definitiva una vez haya regresado de mis vacaciones.

Victoria: ¡Excelente! ¿Alguna otra cosa? Ya creo estar completamente clara con respecto a lo que debo hacer.

Kyle: No, en absoluto. Ahora sí, creo que puedo irme al Caribe sin ninguna preocupación o remordimiento. Ya sabes, nos veremos pronto. Maneja todo esto y cuida la empresa como si fuera tuya. Sé que puedo contar contigo, y que todo estará mejor que como lo dejé. ¡Mucha suerte!

English

Kyle: Well, the big moment has arrived for me to take my well-deserved vacations and step aside from this great business that keeps me busy twenty-four hours a day, seven days a week. As we already discussed, **you're fully in charge of operations for three months.** Prepared?

Victoria: Yes, Kyle, I'm definitely ready. Even so, **I would like us to make one last brief** of **what is expected of me in this new role. I've received training for two months for this moment,** but **I want to cover all the bases.**

Kyle: It's a good initiative, there's no problem if you want to do that. Okay, let's begin. Among your most important responsibilities, **I'm going to need you to oversee personnel management.** Everything that includes **research, screening and contracting,** as well as the **weekly payments and performance.**

Victoria: I understand, that's okay. What other thing would be among **the highest priorities?**

Kyle: You really need to be clear on what I expect in terms of our **sales system.** I want you to familiarize yourself with our workers in this department, with the process they use for the **management of our clients,** as well as **the software we use for the registry of our allies.**

Victoria: Perfect. I had also been mentioned something about **the suppliers and the acquirement of raw material,** no?

Kyle: It's great that you mention it – we must be very clear that it will be one of your large responsibilities to **receive and attend to the people in charge of bringing our raw material,** as well as the necessary resources such as **ingredients for the workers' mess hall, the drinking water for the offices, the cleaning materials and everything related to stationary.** This can easily be forgotten, so please take note.

Victoria: Yes, I'll make sure to have everything **well noted in terms of those goods which are crucial for the company's operation.** I would love to know something: what about the advertising we have in place right now? Will I also be behind all of that?

Kyle: The truth is that yes, **you wouldn't have to create the advertisements or anything similar**, but definitely ensure that it's working and being transmitted on each indicated channel. Whether it's **the advertising on television, radio or on social media**. Please, don't lose sight of those three marketing channels.

Victoria: No, Kyle. I promise you that I'll have my attention on that at all times. **I'll also develop an email marketing strategy**, since it is **one of our weaknesses which could be successfully harnessed** with enough ideas. We have **an audience there with which we can connect**.

Kyle: Excellent suggestion. Let's see, what other aspect can you offer us in this time I'll be absent?

Victoria: Well, I think I could work on **our brand's image**, and on the possibilities of **refreshing our logo and the company slogan. Minimalist logos** are really in right now, and I feel that I could work on the company's personality **so that it can reach more people** who feel identified with it. I have experience in this due to previous jobs where I was the **public relations strategist**, and I could also locate **useful sponsors** with which we could achieve **great commercial deals**.

Kyle: Sounds great! I think it's now time for a change in both things, since we're working with the logo that my father created for the company around thirty-five years ago, as well as a logo which has seemed **obsolete** to me in these current times. Present several ideas, and **I'll give you a definite answer once I've come back** from my holiday.

Victoria: Excellent! Anything else? I believe I'm completely clear now in terms of what I have to do.

Kyle: No, not at all. Now I can definitely go to the Caribbean without any worries or regrets. You know, we'll see each other soon. Manage all of this and **take care of the company as if it were your own**. I know I can count on you, and **that everything will be better than I left it**. Good luck!

MORE FROM LINGO MASTERY

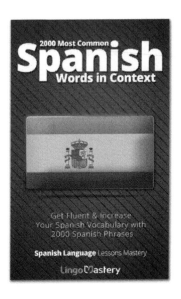

Have you been trying to learn Spanish and simply can't find the way to expand your vocabulary?

Do your teachers recommend you boring textbooks and complicated stories that you don't really understand?

Are you looking for a way to learn the language quicker without taking shortcuts?

If you answered *"Yes!"* to at least one of those previous questions, then this book is for you! We've compiled the **2000 Most Common Words in Spanish,** a list of terms that will expand your vocabulary to levels previously unseen.

Did you know that — according to an important study — learning the top two thousand (2000) most frequently used words will enable you to understand up to **84%** of all non-fiction and **86.1%** of fiction literature and **92.7%** of oral speech? Those are *amazing* stats, and this book will take you even further than those numbers!

In this book:

- A detailed introduction with tips and tricks on how to improve your learning

- A list of **2000** of the most common words in Spanish and their translations

- An example sentence for each word – in both Spanish *and* English

- Finally, a conclusion to make sure you've learned and supply you with a final list of tips

Don't look any further, we've got what you need right here!

In fact, we're ready to turn you into a Spanish speaker...

...are you ready to get involved in becoming one?

Do you know what the hardest thing for a Spanish learner is?

Finding PROPER reading material that they can handle...which is precisely the reason we've written this book!

Teachers love giving out tough, expert-level literature to their students, books that present many new problems to the reader and force them to search for words in a dictionary every five minutes — it's not entertaining, useful or motivating for the student at all, and many soon give up on learning at all!

In this book we have compiled 20 easy-to-read, compelling and fun stories that will allow you to expand your vocabulary and give you the tools to improve your grasp of the wonderful Spanish tongue.

How Spanish Short Stories for Beginners works:

- Each story will involve an important lesson of the tools in the Spanish language (Verbs, Adjectives, Past Tense, Giving Directions, and more), involving an interesting and entertaining story with realistic dialogues and day-to-day situations.

- The summaries follow: a synopsis in Spanish and in English of what you just read, both to review the lesson and for you to see if you understood what the tale was about.

- At the end of those summaries, you'll be provided with a list of the most relevant vocabulary involved in the lesson, as well as slang and sayings that you may not have understood at first glance!

- Finally, you'll be provided with a set of tricky questions in Spanish, providing you with the chance to prove that you learned something in the story. Don't worry if you don't know the answer to any — we will provide them immediately after, but no cheating!

We want you to feel comfortable while learning the tongue; after all, no language should be a barrier for you to travel around the world and expand your social circles!

So look no further! Pick up your copy of **Spanish Short Stories for Beginners** and improve your Spanish right now!

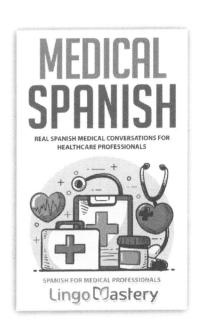

Have you faced a medical emergency with a Spanish-speaking patient and found yourself unable to communicate with them?

Do you want to have the ability to read through Spanish medical texts?

Are you moving to a Spanish-speaking country and need to learn the language on a technical level?

As a healthcare professional, you will come across all types of challenges in your daily work – as if the tasks you face already weren't tough enough, right? - so coping with each and every little thing can be a daunting task.

One of the biggest roadblocks you can hit as a nurse, doctor or other health professional is a language barrier, in which you simply cannot understand or express what needs to be said. Everything slows down, and many times people suffer negative consequences because of it.

For that precise reason, we have produced Medical Spanish: Real Spanish Medical Conversations for Healthcare Professionals to provide you with powerful, up-to-date and necessary tools to master the use of medical Spanish at all levels, from beginner to expert.

With this book:

- Discover essential medical vocabulary, giving you the ability to express many terms that you will use on a day-to-day basis as a healthcare professional.

- Learn to recognize a person's health condition and make a diagnosis based on the information you have.

- Read through over 25 conversations detailing very specific, common situations that any healthcare professional will face, with a resolution to each conflict provided.

- Stay up to date with accurate, modern terminologies and procedures used – all while learning how to express them in Spanish!

- Make use of an incredible learning material that will boost your vocabulary and fluency skills in no-time!

So with that said, all that's left for you is to purchase this book now and begin seeing the advantages that only Medical Spanish: Real Spanish Medical Conversations for Healthcare Professionals can provide you. Good luck!

Is conversational Spanish turning a little too tricky for you? Do you have no idea on how to order a meal or book a room at a hotel?

If your answer to any of the previous questions was 'Yes', then this book is for you!

If there's even been something tougher than learning the grammar rules of a new language, it's finding the way to speak with other people in that tongue. Any student knows this – we can try our best at practicing, but you always want to avoid making embarrassing mistakes or not getting your message through correctly.

'How do I get out of this situation?' many students ask themselves, to no avail, but no answer is forthcoming.

Until now.

We have compiled **MORE THAN ONE HUNDRED** Spanish Stories for Beginners along with their translations, allowing new Spanish speakers to have the necessary tools to begin studying how to set a meeting, rent a car or tell a doctor that they don't feel well! We're not wasting time here with conversations that don't go anywhere: if you want to know how to solve problems (while learning a ton of Spanish along the way, obviously), this book is for you!

How Conversational Spanish Dialogues works:

- Each new chapter will have a fresh, new story between two people who wish to solve a common, day-to-day issue that you will surely encounter in real life.

- A Spanish version of the conversation will take place first, followed by an English translation. This ensures that you fully understood just what it was that they were saying!

- Before and after the main section of the book, we shall provide you with an introduction and conclusion that will offer you important strategies, tips and tricks to allow you to get the absolute most out of this learning material.

- That's about it! Simple, useful and incredibly helpful; you will **NOT** need another conversational Spanish book once you have begun reading and studying this one!

We want you to feel comfortable while learning the tongue; after all, no language should be a barrier for you to travel around the world and expand your social circles!

So look no further!

Pick up your copy of **Conversational Spanish Dialogues** and start learning Spanish right now!

CONCLUSION

We may have reached the end of *Business Spanish: Learn Conversational Spanish For Business Professionals*, but the good news is that you are still far from being done in your Spanish language learning!

Created for you, the daring entrepreneur and business owner that helps make the world's finance operate like a well-oiled machine, this book was created not only to allow you to learn how to communicate with similar people in the world of business, but also for you to develop your interpersonal skills in terms of regular situations which you will find yourself in. Whether it's getting a job at an important company, firing an inefficient employee or dominating a sales meeting, this book will be your closest ally.

But what else can we provide you with, in these last couple of pages before we say goodbye?

It's simple: you have the book in front of you and you've now read it... but have you learned to harness all of its contents and use them to the best of your abilities? Doubtful. Therefore, as a parting gift, we are providing you with a list of strategies that will allow you to crush any business encounters that you need to experience in Spanish, boost your ability to connect with customers in the Latin American region, and communicate effectively with your Spanish-speaking associates.

Don't miss out on these amazing tactics that will definitely lead you to getting the most of this book!

5 Strategies for Businessmen and Businesswomen Studying Spanish

1. Try reading in Spanish as much as you can

One book isn't all you can lean on as a Spanish student (or language student in general). You need to complement your main sources of learning (such as this book) with other written materials that can provide you with additional vocabulary, present you with additional common situations, and help you clear up all of the more complicated terminology that you may need to translate.

Acquiring reading practice will be crucial if you want to dominate the Spanish tongue, so prepare to enhance your learning by consuming plenty of written materials.

2. Don't give up and revert back to English

Don't lose hope in learning just because you hit a few obstacles! Nobody said it would be easy. In fact, the hardest moments in language learning are: number one, getting started, and number two, getting past the basics. Believe us when we tell you – if you can surpass these two tough stages of the game, then you're halfway on your way to becoming fluent in Spanish.

Motivate yourself with rewards, set a diary, log or blog which documents your progress, and set realistic goals each month so that you can grow steadily!

3. Vocabulary is KEY in learning: value it!

Honestly, some language students believe that learning a tongue is about knowing all the rules and pronouncing well... *wrong!* Most of what you'll know in a language will be based on the amount of vocabulary you're familiar with.

This is the precise reason why we've added the vocabulary lists before every single story. It's not just a fun tool that you have – it's a way for you to acquire the tools that you'll use to communicate on a daily basis with your clients, associates, employees and superiors. Don't waste the opportunity to help your language skills grow with vocabulary practice!

4. Reading while Listening – an amazing language-learning method you can apply

If you think reading is a fascinating way of learning a new tongue and listening is another great way, why not to do both simultaneously? Important studies made by linguistic specialists have discovered that reading while listening is one of the most impressive language-learning methods for students of all ages, with the ability to boost fluency levels beyond that of any other method, as well as enhance pronunciation, comprehension and obviously, save time for those using the two methods separately.

With audiobooks (such as the one created for this book) you can find the best of both worlds. Feel free to acquire other similar audiobooks for similar results and look on YouTube and similar learning channels for methods of reading while listening (RwL) that will take your Spanish to new levels.

5. Take some time to practice with your fellow businessmen and businesswomen

Let's face it – the best way to learn a new language, besides using all of the strategies mentioned above, is by learning it with someone at your side to work and practice with. The results you can achieve with a friend or colleague just trump all of those that you will obtain on your own, considering how effective teamwork can be in these situations.

If you believe that you can find someone with a level of commitment similar to yours, who is willing to spend time studying with you and who is patient enough to help you with your mistakes and listen to you helping them with theirs, then you're on your way to forming an excellent partnership – or who knows, maybe even a study group!

Now, finally, we have truly reached the end of **Business Spanish: Real Spanish Business Conversations for Businessmen and Businesswomen** – we hope you have found great value in this book and wish you plenty of luck. Don't be afraid to fail: read these stories as many times as you need and apply all of the strategies we have recommended. You will be speaking Business Spanish like a pro *very* soon!

Don't stop learning, student... no matter what!

THE END

Made in the USA
Las Vegas, NV
18 October 2023

79298111R00109